WEDDING SPEECHES

Also available:

Sample Social Speeches

Right Joke For The Right Occasion

Best Man's Duties

Public Speaker's Joke Book

WEDDING SPEECHES

(Example speeches for bride's father, groom, best man and others)

Gordon Stretch

RIGHT WAY

Printed and bound in Great Britain by Cox & Wyman Ltd., Reading, Berkshire.

The *Right Way* series is published by Elliot Right Way Books, Brighton Road, Lower Kingswood, Tadworth, Surrey, KT20 6TD, U.K. For information about our company and the other books we publish, visit our web site at www.right-way.co.uk

CONTENTS

To Mum and Dad

PART 1
INTRODUCTION

A wedding is an occasion that should be enjoyed by all — even those giving the speeches! But, many of us have never spoken to a gathering before, and the thought of standing in front of a group of people fills us with horror. To overcome this, I have collected together 65 example speeches. One or other of these is bound to suit your wedding — whether it's the first wedding of a young couple or the "second-time around" for two people with adult children.

There are example speeches for the three traditional wedding speakers — 12 for the bride's father, 15 for the bridegroom and 15 for the best man. At some weddings the bride's father may not be able to attend (he may be ill, or have left home, or have died) or he may just prefer to leave the speechmaking to someone else, so I have included eight speeches that other members of the bride's family (the bride's uncle, grandfather or brother) could give on his behalf.

Going beyond the usual three speeches, it is becoming increasingly common for others to have their say, including the ladies. So among the 15 extra speeches in Part 6 are some which could be given by the bride herself or her sister or mother.

Each speech is a complete entity. However, to suit your own personal situation you may like to adapt a speech and incorporate in it appropriate material from any of the other speeches.

It's a good idea to confer with your fellow speakers before the wedding to make sure you're not duplicating the same material or using the same jokes! In fact I have produced some pairs of speeches which can be used together: see pages 29 and 179; 32 and 140; 38 and 152; 41 and 110; and 104 and 155.

When composing your speech, do consider the feelings of the people about whom you are talking; make sure you don't say anything that could be misinterpreted (unless that's your intention) or ridicule someone to such an extent that they are hurt by your words. Your speech should make everyone laugh — including the person who might be the butt of your jokes!

How to deliver the speech

After you've compiled your speech, make clear notes large enough to enable you to read them at a quick glance without having to keep bending down.

Rehearse out loud facing a mirror. This will give you confidence and the required practice in the proper form of delivery for each part of the speech, including looking cheerful and smiling when appropriate. Stand up straight and look around your imagined audience so that this will come easily during the delivery, and you will be able to concentrate on putting the life into the speech itself.

If time is too short for you to learn your speech, using merely guiding notes, and you are obliged to read it all out, then you will have to write it all out in a formal way, differently from the free-and-easy spontaneity of manner used in this book. If you do write your whole speech out, leave ample space between the lines: this will make it easier to read and save you from losing your place.

Above all, don't worry about your speech; you're giving it at a wedding and your audience is bound to be good-natured — many of them will have been in a similar position and will sympathise with any nerves that you might have.

The Best Man generally acts as toastmaster at the wedding ceremony and he calls on the first speaker when he considers the time is right. I give below the traditional order of speeches at the reception:

1. The Bride's Father — at the end of his speech he toasts the health and happiness of the bride and groom.

2. The Bridegroom replies on behalf of his wife and himself. At the end of his speech he toasts the bridesmaids.

3. The Best Man replies on the bridesmaids' behalf. If there are any telemessages or cards from absent family or friends, he will read these out at the end of his speech.

4. If any others are going to speak, they would usually speak now. Then "the cutting of the cake" may follow, if it didn't take place before the speeches.

PART 2
BRIDE'S FATHER'S SPEECHES

BRIDE'S FATHER No. 1

Whenever I've been thinking aloud about what I'd like to say on this happy occasion, the wife has kept chipping in with, "Don't forget to thank everybody for coming." There am I, trying to work out something grandiose to fasten your attention on my every word, and Mary has to deflate my mood with (MOCKINGLY) "Don't forget to thank everybody for coming!" I can't imagine that Winston Churchill had that trouble when he was preparing one of his important speeches to Parliament. Fancy him having to say, "Thank you all for coming," to satisfy Mrs. Churchill. Anyway, to save myself getting into trouble, thank you all for coming.

Of course my thanks would have been there even if I had overlooked to express them. It's lovely to be surrounded by family and friends at the same time, and to bask in the atmosphere of an event like this. Weddings are invariably very happy occasions, and this one is no exception.

Having thanked you all for being here, I'd like to say a special "thank you" to John. Yes, I do refer to Jane's John. You see, it is not only Jane and John's day, but Mary's and mine too, because we have gained as a son someone of whom we are greatly fond, and both of us are so grateful to him for coming here as the bridegroom.

With our other children we had to do things like forever changing nappies, and getting up in the night to find out why they were crying, and when they were a little older buy them ice creams to shut them up. With John we haven't had to change a single nappy. He's come to us as a young man ready-made.

I don't like the mouthful "son-in-law". It sounds as though "son" is qualified and the person concerned is a step away. Certainly for Mary and myself the "in-law" tag is merely legal terminology irrelevant to the relationship between John and ourselves. What makes things so much more joyful for us is

13

knowing that our dear Jane has this young man as a husband. In the nicest way we can say that they deserve each other.

What we find gratifying also is that John's parents feel the same about Jane. They have taken her to their hearts and they must now feel that they have gained a lovely daughter.

With such all-round harmony we feel thrice blessed ... I don't think I've ever said that before — "thrice". It's surprising what you come out with in a speech ... It sounds as if we've had triplets.

A word of caution to the bridegroom, however, will not go amiss. As an old married man — well, it can make you feel old, even if you are only middle-aged — I can speak from experience to this freshman here and warn him what he'll be up against. I didn't think it wise to say anything before he'd gone through the wedding ceremony, in case he changed his mind. There's something you'll have to learn to live with, John, because no man has yet found a remedy for it, and that is the unfathomable female mind. It can be summed up by one simple instance.

A woman bought her husband two ties for his birthday, a red one and a blue one. He was undecided which one to wear at his party that evening, but he appeared in the red one. As soon as his wife saw him she said, "Oh, you're wearing the red tie. Don't you like the blue one?"

There's no way you can win. However, forewarned is forearmed and now John is forearmed, in that at least he knows what to expect.

Don't worry too much, John. Mary and I have known Jane for a lot longer than you have, and things shouldn't be quite as bad as that. In any case, with your resourcefulness you would probably do something like wearing two ties at the same time. I've done stranger things than that to keep the peace with Mary, but if you and Jane have half the happiness in your married life that we have had in ours, then yours will be a very happy marriage indeed.

It is my pleasure to ask everyone to drink to that.

Ladies and gentlemen, would you please join me in a toast to the health and happiness of Jane and John.

(IMMEDIATELY AFTER TOAST) Oh, and by the way, just to make doubly sure, thank you all for coming.

BRIDE'S FATHER No. 2
(Bride a waitress)

Well, here we go again. This is the third wedding speech I've made. At the first of them the bridegroom was one of the most handsome you could wish to see. His bride must have been the envy of all the ladies that set eyes on him. She surely was a very lucky lady. That young man has not lost any of his charm with the passing years. But that's enough about me.

The second wedding was that of one of our daughters. Now it is another daughter, so this is my second speech as the bride's father.

There are three ladies in my life that I am proud of and who are a source of immense happiness to me. The firstcomer was Mary. The second to appear was our dear daughter, Joan, and the third was another dear daughter, our Jane, today's bride.

One thing leads to another, and that's certainly true of a wedding. The wedding of Mary and myself has led to two more weddings already. All three weddings have had one thing in common for me. The feeling of pride that I had at my own wedding came back to me when Joan was married, and it's come back again today.

Until Joan married we didn't have a son, but we gained one in Alan. It was as though our family had suddenly increased. Now the same thing is happening again. We're gaining another son.

When it was just the two of us, Mary and myself, I felt outnumbered. A man does, you know. In any argument (and I do mean friendly argument, not a quarrel) between man and wife, the man does feel outnumbered, because the wife says twice as much as the man. (John, I hope you're listening carefully. This is being explained for your benefit.) Now, the reason that the wife says twice as much as the man is because the wife carries on talking while the man is silently trying to fathom the logic of the statements that she's just made. It dawned on me too late in my married life that all the time I'd spent trying to find that elusive logic had been wasted. There wasn't any logic.

When Joan was old enough to stand on her own verbal feet, the outnumbering ratio was three to one, and when Jane was old enough, it was four to one. With the acquisition of two more males, the balance is tipping in my favour when we're all together.

Mary and I are delighted that Jane, like her sister before her, has made a splendid match. Jane and John have known each other long enough to be able to start their married life together happy in the knowledge that they get on famously together. They're alike in their natures, active and eager to have a go at anything.

When Jane was only in her infancy she took up the violin, and after a few minutes of determined effort we managed to get it off her. What made us do that was not so much the sound of her playing as the sound of Stradivari turning in his grave.

She couldn't wait to take driving lessons. I knuckled under to her persuasion to give her some instruction as soon as she was old enough. Have you ever seen anybody do a three-point turn at 45 miles an hour? Naturally Jane's become more skilful since then. She can now do a three-point turn at 60 miles an hour.

She knew nothing about the requirements of the driving test on that first practice. I said, "Quick! Do an emergency stop!" She said, "What's the emergency?" I said, "I want to get out."

I've heard it said that some people live by their wits and others by their common sense. Jane lives by both. This gives her the advantage to deal with any crisis. And believe me, in her job as a waitress, from the tales that are told, this is a godsend. When the chef's at fault, it's still the waitress that has to deal with the complaint. She served to one man a bowl of something piled up like a pyramid. When he protested, she pointed out to him that he had asked for the thick soup.

Her resourcefulness has saved the situation many a time. A woman ordered some Emmental cheese. They hadn't any left, so Jane cut a chunk of cheddar and drilled holes in it.

The menu contained a long list — "eggs on toast", "beans

on toast", "cheese on toast", "sardines on toast", and so on. One day the equipment overheated and Jane added "toast on fire".

John, my son, you're going to be in capable hands.

May I say in conclusion that Mary and I are happy to welcome into our fold two nice people not yet mentioned, but without whom John wouldn't be here. No, I don't mean the best man and the taxi driver, but John's parents, already our valued friends.

Ladies and gentlemen, it is my privilege and pleasure finally to propose the toast to the continuing health and happiness of Jane and John.

BRIDE'S FATHER No. 3

(Bride a shop assistant)

In the normal way I should be apprehensive about standing up and making a speech. This occasion, however, is different, and the difference is that there are many thoughts that I am only too eager to express which are, as it were, close to home.

With some speeches that are compulsory we may have to grope for things to say, but a proud and happy father can find his mind overflowing with thoughts on such an occasion as this.

When I settled down to make some notes, putting my thoughts into some sort of order, no end of variety of things popped into my head to convey to you the rich experience that Mary and I have enjoyed in bringing up Jane and having her with us right until today, when she embarks upon life in her own home. Yes, so many things, but don't worry, you're only going to hear a few of them, because this is a wedding reception and not my one-man speech day.

Jane has been a wonderful daughter to Mary and myself and at this point of our parting with her into another's keeping we thank her for all the twenty-one unbroken years of joy that she has given us. I know that she's twenty-three, but we don't count the first two years because then she used to wake us up at all times of the night.

The delightful little girl that we found ourselves with went on to become a delightful big girl with many admirers and many suitors, all but one of whom, of course, were destined to fall by the wayside. With Jane's kind heart she would have done her best to let them down lightly. She's always been a thoughtful girl and she's always been a happy girl. What more could parents ask for, even though Mary and I did get much, much more?

What more, indeed, could the customers who enter her shop ask for in the person who serves them? We all know what a difference it makes when a sales assistant is of a pleasant, friendly disposition and tries to be helpful. It doesn't matter whether you're buying slippers or kippers, the person who serves you either adds to or detracts from the quality of your life for that short while, and it's the Janes of this world that add to the quality of our lives.

I'm reminded of a young lad who started work in a grocer's shop and all he knew about food was that it was something you ate. A regular customer went in on the lad's first day. She'd brought some cheese back and she said to him, "This smells." He said, "It's supposed to," and she said, "It's not supposed to smell smelly." He said, "Well, leave it with us and we'll see if we can make it better."

I'm sure that kind of service is a far cry from our Jane's early days behind a counter.

John, to turn to your good self, Jane's mother and I have been on cloud nine ever since you chose us as your mother-in-law and father-in-law. You can relax and rest assured that Jane's mum will not live up to the traditional image of a mother-in-law. I know her too well for that. Just because she slighted you for not letting her chaperone Jane on the honeymoon don't get the wrong impression of how she's going to be in the future.

Ladies and gentlemen, I believe that I'm running out of time, if I'm to allow others to speak, so I'll try to be brief.

I hinted at the start that the wealth of happiness that Jane has given to Mary and myself could not be summed up adequately in a short speech. I have proved myself right. There is, however, something that Mary and I should like emphasised before I finish, and that is that today we honour not Jane alone, whom we can say so much about because we've known her intimately all her life, but also the splendid lad that we have known for only a fraction of that time, namely John.

Furthermore, we wish to say a very warm welcome into the family to John's mum and dad, and indeed all their family.

Now, Jane and John, it is to both of you that we are going to raise our glasses and wish you health and happiness in your future as man and wife.

Ladies and gentlemen, will you please join me in a toast to Jane and John.

BRIDE'S FATHER No. 4

A wedding is always thought of as a bride and groom's special day, but it's also a special day for their parents, because it's an important event in their own married life.

If it's the first time that one of their offspring is getting married, then it's a milestone. Now, what is a milestone? I suppose we've all seen Dick Whittington in the pantomime. There is Dick, consulting an AA map, trying to work out how much farther it is to London, and there's a giant cat miaowing and pointing a paw at a stone pillar by the wayside, on which is shown the number of miles to go. A milestone marks the point of completion of a certain distance on a journey.

This has become a metaphor for reaching a stage in life or in one of life's undertakings. In Dick Whittington's day a milestone in the literal sense was something that tempted the weary foot-traveller to stop and rest awhile, undo his packed lunch and entertain thoughts of what lay ahead.

Today a milestone has been reached by some of us here, and all of us have sat down and eaten the packed lunch. I hasten to add that I'm still speaking figuratively when I refer to our delicious meal in that way.

For Mary and myself it's the completion of looking after a child of ours under our own roof. We have brought up that child and taken care of her to the best of our ability until she has become mature enough and prepared enough to start her own married life, outside our keeping. So at one and the same time it's a milestone in the lives of Mary and myself on the one hand and of Jane on the other. That's not all of course, because the same situation is reflected in John and his parents.

As we six travellers pause on our journey I suspect that the hearts and minds of Jane and John are too overflowing with joyful thoughts of the married life ahead of them for there to be any room for serious reflection on the past. That's good. It's we other four who look back. Jane and John rejoice because they have just gained each other. We parents have reached the end of that part of our lives during which we had the joy of the close company of our respective children, and our jubilation at today's event can be touched with a sense of loss.

I don't need to expand on that because you will all know what I mean. I mention it only as a tribute to Jane from Mary and myself — a thanks for the immense happiness that it has given us to have her as a daughter.

Now, I took as my text for today the career of Dick Whittington in pantomime. In real life he went on to great prosperity. My life before meeting Mary was more like a pantomime, and this continued in one respect after the milestone of our wedding. I simply changed from Dick Whittington and became Baron Hardup.

My grandmother used to say, "A penny bun costs you twopence when you're courting." It didn't cost her twopence. It cost granddad twopence. I discovered that when you've been married a few years and have a family a penny bun could cost you fourpence. Then there was the cat to feed. I suppose I should be grateful that our cat wasn't as big as Dick Whittington's.

Although material prosperity does help to make life a little more comfortable, I am more concerned at this particular time to toast the good fortune of the bride and groom. It is the wish for health and happiness in their married life that I would like us all to keep uppermost in our minds.

Mary and I are truly grateful to all of you for joining us in this happy celebration, and in spite of what I've said about my own plight you needn't put too much money in my hat on your way out — just whatever you can comfortably afford. Really I exaggerated about being Baron Hardup. I've managed to pay for this wedding without strain. It's Jane's sister's wedding that I have to start saving for now. That's why my hat will be there at the door.

So there we are, ladies and gentlemen. That pleasurable moment has arrived when I ask you all to stand and join me in that toast to the health and happiness of bride and groom.

BRIDE'S FATHER No. 5

(Groom a policeman)

When Mary first told me that Jane and John were serious about each other I was elated. It meant that the burden of the wedding speech that would fall upon me sooner or later would be lightened. Because John was a policeman I should have something to go on.

I started to list all the puns I could think of to do with the police. That was quite a time ago. As that once dreaded moment has arrived when I stand before you guests to start my speech, I have in front of me that list of puns. (PICK UP VERY SMALL PIECE OF PAPER) I've got them written on the back of this receipt I had from Sainsbury's for a jar of onions and two packets of cornflakes.

I thought that would *arrest* your attention. (PICK UP PEN AND CROSS OUT "ARREST") That's the first one gone. I'll drop the other two out when you don't expect it, so listen for them. Would you believe how difficult it was trying to think of more puns!

Anyway, it would have been comforting for Mary and me to know that the man that Jane was going to marry was a policeman even if we hadn't met him, because in our view policemen are solid, reliable and level-headed people and very responsible. They go out there on the streets at all hours of the day and night for our protection and assistance, exposing themselves to abuse and danger.

In the case of young members of the force like John our admiration is heightened, because the dangers that have to be faced are regrettably much greater than a generation ago. It takes courage nowadays to serve the public in the capacity that John has chosen, and the young men − and women − who enter into this deserve our recognition.

This means that the fact alone of John's vocation would be

reassuring for Mary and me because of significant things that it would tell us straight away. However, we now know John also as an individual, and everything that we learn about his character first-hand makes us more happy for Jane, to have such a fine partner, and for ourselves, having such a fine son-in-law. (No, "son-in-*law*" wasn't intentional!)

John is ambitious and is prepared to persevere for promotion, and he has told us that no matter how long it takes, he will *plod* on. (TAKE PAPER AND PEN, CROSS OUT "PLOD") That's two down and one to go. It was "plod", for anybody who hadn't noticed.

There's an old saying, "A policeman's lot is not a nappy one." Well, Mary and I hope that to some extent it will be, because we like to visualise Jane and John's back garden with a clothesline punctuated with nappies as well as police socks.

One thing, John, if you have as large a family as Mary and I wish on you, there'll be no cause for anxiety. By then you will have had plenty of practice at crowd control. If you forget which one is which, just remember that Jane is (E.G. the tall, fair-haired one who wears glasses).

Jane has never been any trouble to us, John, and I don't think we've been a trouble to her. Isn't that right, Jane? Of course there's always a difficult phase that parents have to endure with a daughter .... from about the age of three to twenty-three. You know how rebellious a girl can be when she wants to be free from parental restriction and have her fling. Her parents naturally worry about her staying out late at night and mixing with heaven knows who. However, I was exaggerating when I said three to twenty-three. It definitely wasn't that with Jane. By the time she was four that phase was over.

When Mary and I were at Jane and John's stage there was still a term used for a baby which might surprise some young people. It was called a gift. We looked upon Jane as a gift when she was born and we've continued to look at her like that ever since. She has been to us a cherished gift. Today we entrust that gift to another's care, confident in the soundness of that care.

(GLANCE DOWN) Oh, I nearly forgot to exhaust my list of puns, and there's a bonus one in this. If they have a red-haired child its *nickname* could be "Coppernob" ..... I think I'm getting into the swing of being a policeman's father-in-law.

Ladies and gentlemen, to wish the happy couple good fortune in their life of taking care of each other, would you please join the toast which it is my privilege to propose, namely the health and happiness of the bride and groom.

BRIDE'S FATHER No. 6

It doesn't seem long since I stood here and made my first speech as a bride's father. It was a task that I had looked forward to with mixed feelings, and there must be some of the gentlemen here today who will know from experience what I mean.

When you are not a habitual speechmaker it can give you the jitters because you're going to be in the spotlight carrying out a performance that you're not adequately practised in, and you're anxious about remembering most of what you want to say.

On the other hand there is the pleasurable anticipation of having a unique opportunity to express to your family and friends — and that includes newly-acquired family and friends — the feelings that you have as the father of a lovely young lady on her special day.

At the end of that first speech that I made I proposed the traditional toast to the health and happiness of the bride and groom. It worked. Kate and Ron have been as happy as biddies, whatever they are. I don't know what magic potion was slipped into our glasses by some kind fairy when we drank that toast, but our wishes were well and truly fulfilled.

Mary and I were excited when Kate announced that she was getting engaged to Ron, because we had secretly kept our fingers crossed that this would happen. We had seen clearly that he was Mr. Right, and we wanted him in the family.

What I'm leading up to is that on this occasion, Jane and John's wedding, I have been less apprehensive about my spell in the spotlight because of my confidence that their partnership is going to follow in the wake of Kate and Ron's. Even if I make a hash of things and get booed off the stage, it's of little consequence in relation to that.

It is going to be history repeated. I don't mean me getting booed off the stage, because that didn't happen. I mean the success of Jane and John's marriage. There is, of course, a little sadness at the severing of the umbilical cord, but that passes. Mary and I can rejoice that the second of our lovely daughters has made a match with her Mr. Right, and indeed, as with her sister, in doing so she has brought more welcome people into the family.

Now, what can we tell John about our Jane now that he's well and truly hooked and it's too late for him to have any second thoughts about marrying her? He can't have heard everything about her — not from us, anyway, because we were on our guard not to put him off her.

Perhaps we should say nothing so that he can at least have today in blissful ignorance. He'll find out all in good time.

However, on the theme of the happy state of affairs in our own family circle it is with an inward sigh of relief that Mary and I have contemplated our own fortune. Just to point up what can happen with the break-up of marriages, there was a couple who were joined together in some kind of matrimony, holy or otherwise, after both having been married previously.

One day the man was looking through the window into their back garden and he said to the woman, "You know my kids?" She said, "Yes." He said, "And you know your kids?" She said, "Yes." He said, "Well, they're fighting our kids."

It only remains for me to propose the toast to Jane and John, and as you drink imagine that while I've been on my feet that fairy has been on the wing, whipping round invisibly, dropping more of that same potion into our glasses.

Ladies and gentlemen, I give you the toast to the health and happiness of Jane and John.

BRIDE'S FATHER No. 7
(Whirlwind engagement)

When I became aware that this day was fast approaching and I felt it was time to start organising my speech as the bride's father, I was reminded of what I'd been told about another man in the same situation.

He'd popped into the bedroom to change and he took advantage to spend a moment rehearsing part of his speech in front of the mirror. There he was, spreading his hands and gesticulating, when his wife overheard him and looked in. She said, "Who arc you talking to?" He said, "I'm rehearsing my speech for Saturday." She said, "Well, they won't hear a word you say. They'll be too fascinated seeing you standing there in your underpants." He said, "That's a good idea. It's one way of making a memorable speech."

Well, I don't aspire to make a memorable speech for an occasion like this, even if I could. That's not what we're here for. I only wish to use the opportunity to express to you my feelings — and Mary's — about Jane and John becoming man and wife. We couldn't be more happy.

Jane and John had known each other for only a short time before they became engaged. In many cases when that happens and the couple lose no time in putting wedding arrangements into operation it can be a good thing that churches are booked so far in advance that there's a long delay before the wedding can take place. It gives the couple a cooling-off period during which one of them at least may conclude that getting married is a mistake. (PAUSE, THEN HASTILY, AS AN AFTERTHOUGHT) I don't mean they conclude that getting married at all is a mistake, I mean the couple in question marrying each other.

You might think that Mary and I, of all people, would be the anxious ones, and if it had been any other man except John, then yes, we should have been ill at ease.

As it happened, John was a person that we were able to know very quickly, just as Jane had found, and the person that Mary and I came to know, we liked very much indeed. We recognised in him the qualities that he had in common with Jane, and it was clear that they were made for each other. They are two of a kind and fate brought them together.

The interesting thing is that their early decision to marry was not the result of being impulsive. Those who know Jane well enough also know of her cautious nature, and the same goes for John. No, they were like two pieces of a jigsaw puzzle that matched each other. I dare say that Shakespeare would have expressed that more poetically, but it should suffice to illustrate the point.

Well, time has passed and our confidence has been justified. The lovebirds have deepened their relationship and it's bedrock firm. (PAUSE, THEN TURN TO JANE AND JOHN) I'm sorry, I shouldn't have used that word. There was no innuendo intended. You've got me flustered now ..... or rather I've got myself flustered. Now, where was I? ..... I know where I wish I was at the moment. I don't know about a blushing bride. I think you've got a blushing bride's father. My speech might be a memorable one after all — memorable just for one gaffe.

Already I have visions of John in seventy years' time saying to Jane, (SQUEAKY OLD VOICE) "Do you remember your silly old duffer of a dad at our wedding reception saying something about our bedrock relationship?" .... and five minutes later Jane saying, (VERY HIGH-PITCHED SQUEAKY OLD VOICE) "No, I don't even remember my silly old duffer of a dad." .... and John saying, "I still can't work out how he knew about it."

Sorry about that. I had better get back to the point of my speech which, after all, is to toast the bride and groom. There is much more that I should like to say, but my time is rationed, so forgive me if I appear to end abruptly.

I will simply ask you now please to stand and join with me in the traditional toast.

Here's to the health and happiness of Jane and John.

BRIDE'S FATHER No. 8

(Bride a "modern miss", already living with groom)
(Relates to "Extra" speech no. 10, on page 179.)

If ever I encounter an old friend that I haven't spoken to for a year or two, and we're catching up on each other's lives, I'm invariably asked about Jane, with the implied question, "What's she like?" My short answer is that she's a typical "modern miss".

What volumes are spoken in that phrase! ... Some of you might be thinking, "What a multitude of sins it covers!" but I'm not going to be tactless enough to say that!

Now, what does it mean? What do I mean by it? Thinking about this has made me realise how long the phrase has been used, to my recollection. I remember it from decades ago, so with changing fashion, a "modern miss" of today must be different from one of yesteryear. One from forty years ago would appear old-fashioned today.

So to be a full-blooded "modern miss" at any given time means being right up to date with the latest fashions in dress, behaviour, customs and attitudes. To me, central to it also is a rebellion against convention, and a liberation from restriction. The momentum of this rebellion is still with us.

So, Jane, you know what you are — or were — because you are now no longer a "miss". You're a "modern Mrs.".

Now that you're in your twenties you are relatively (and I emphasise "relatively") staid. I mean, today's really "with-it" teenage girl daubs herself with half a pound of make-up, whizzes off to late-night parties just when her parents are going to bed, changes her hairstyle and her boyfriend twice a week and indulges in marathon telephone calls sponsored by her father. Her bedroom walls are covered with huge pictures of weird young men sporting guitars, and her idea of a quiet evening at home is to prance about to pop records played loudly enough to make her granddad rejoice to discover that he's not totally deaf after all. One saving grace is that her skirts at least show that she's wearing knickers.

However, what I'm coming to is that we all, by and large, conform to the outward fashions of our own sex and age group. Notice that I say outward fashions. Basic values are a different thing, and they're what matter.

Practices that are the norm in one society can appear eccentric or outrageous to the members of another. Two different societies can be contemporary, but in different parts of the world, or they can be in the very same location, but in different eras. Just think how shocked our Victorian forebears would be if they saw what we get up to today. Well, what you get up to. I don't know about me.

Anyway, the pace of change has accelerated in recent times, and people in my generation can see wide differences within our own lifetime, and ones which we are bemused by.

Jane and John are in the younger generation, and they followed the now common custom of a trial marriage. With us older folk it can still be a reflex action to raise our eyebrows every time we hear of that happening, but I doubt if you'll see many raised eyebrows amongst the younger generation. Their attitudes have been conditioned differently from ours.

What I want to say is that our instinctive conditioned reactions are not necessarily a guide to what is right and what is wrong — precisely because they are conditioned.

Jane and John are an example of two sensible people who did not lightly (if I may use a telling expression) "shack-up" together. It was because they believed in the dignity of marriage that they wanted to be sure that a marriage between them, if it were entered into, would be a happy one.

Now I'll tell you something else. John's had an exhaustive trial run as a son-in-law. He's passed the test with flying colours. That's what makes Mary and me so happy, that he and Jane have proved to themselves by experience that they are compatible, as they had hoped, and have progressed to marriage.

We welcome John today as a permanent member of the family. Mary and I were relieved and excited when Jane and John said they knew for sure that all was well between them and they planned to marry. We had kept our fingers crossed, because we had become so fond of John and we looked upon him as a son that we had gained. It would have been a sad day indeed if Jane and John had decided that they were not for each other, and would go their separate ways.

I can't help thinking that I'm recounting a fairy tale, and John's parents had a stake in the issue as well. I feel like saying, "and the princess married her prince and they all lived happily ever after."

You know, it's customary for the bride's father to flaunt his wisdom about marriage by publicly passing on advice to the newlyweds. It would be farcical for me to do that. *I've* been asking *John* for advice.

Ladies and gentlemen, would you join me in the toast to our happy pair for their continued health and happiness. Jane and John.

BRIDE'S FATHER No. 9

(Bride a secretary)
(Relates to Best Man's speech no 10, on page 140.)

Before I embark upon a few well-chosen words about my daughter, I should like to attend to some other points, which might otherwise be neglected. *You* might forgive my omissions, but if I overlook certain courtesies and acknowledgements, I stand to get my ears boxed when I get home.

Firstly, Mary and I extend a very warm welcome to all of you to this very special family celebration. We find great pleasure in formally welcoming John into the family. I say "formally", because he's already made himself at home with us and to all intents and purposes has long been in the family. If I can court danger for a moment, I may say, John, that now you're actually married to Jane, you're well and truly in it.

Mary and I are also extremely happy in the cementing of ties between John's family and ours.

Now, Jane, you'll probably be more interested than anyone to hear what I say in the next few minutes, because it's about you.

Much of what Jane is and does is paralleled in her occupation as a secretary. In fact, it has been greatly to the advantage of her mum and dad that when she has come home from work, she hasn't been able to stop being a secretary.

It's interesting to reflect on the innumerable and varied qualities that can come into play daily in the course of that occupation. There are all kinds of challenges popping up.

The job title "secretary" can seem colourless compared with, for example, "air hostess". It's a bit like "housewife". But a housewife can be a self-seeking female who's married a wealthy man in order to live in luxurious ease or she can be an old woman living in a shoe, with so many children that she doesn't know what to do — apart from attending a family planning clinic.

Yes, a secretary is a common enough occupation, but what makes all the difference is the character and the talents that are brought to it. A busy executive relies on a good secretary, and to be a good secretary, a woman has to be an "all-rounder", and always on the ball.

She may be engrossed in a task when there's a phone call for the boss from somebody that she, in her wisdom, knows that he wouldn't want to speak to at that particular time. Quick thinking and imagination are called for if, like Jane, she has scruples, and doesn't use the easy way out by telling a blatant lie. She may start with, "It's a bit tricky for him to take the call at the moment," and if the caller persists, she may add, again without stating a lie, something like, "Aren't you getting the earthquake very badly where you are, then?" and call, "Hold that wall up, somebody, while I'm on the phone!"

Sometimes the boss's lady friend might telephone and that can call for instant ingenuity if his wife's called in at the office and she's nearby. The secretary might say in a stage whisper, "I can't discuss it now because his wife might overhear. He wants the flowers to be a surprise for her."

When his wife's gone she informs her boss what's happened and orders a bouquet to be sent to his wife with the message, "I just couldn't wait till your birthday."

John, you're going to enjoy the benefit of all this prowess in your marriage. You'll not only have a wife, but a built-in, unpaid secretary who will smooth your path besides sweeping it.

Jane will take care of mundane matters, so your mind will be unfettered and free to fly into higher realms — at least, if the experience of Mary and me is anything to go by. While our dear Jane was with us, we wallowed in the luxury of having a self-appointed servant. We came to depend on her too much. When she left home it took us three days to find the pantry.

A man came to the door wanting money for the milk. We thought it was free. Mary said to me one afternoon, "It's about time we made the bed." I said, "Why?" She said, "It hasn't been done for a fortnight."

You'll discover, John, that our loss is your gain.

However, we're not complaining, because we've gained you, and we can still look forward to Jane popping in as often as

possible and making herself at home just as if she still lived there.
In other words, paying the milkman, making our bed, and so on.

On that happy note I should like to round off by asking you
all to stand, please, to toast Jane and John's health and happiness
as man and secretarial wife.

Ladies and gentlemen, Jane and John.

BRIDE'S FATHER No. 10

(Bride a quiet type, bank clerk, already living with groom)

When there's a discussion about another person, it's sometimes rounded off by a charitable, "Ah, well. It takes all sorts to make a world." That tells us that the subject of the discussion is deemed to be either a reprobate or an eccentric.

If I approached two people I knew and one was saying, "Ah, well. It takes all sorts to make a world," and then, on spotting me, they said, "Hello, Frank! We were just talking about you," I should feel distinctly uneasy — probably with good reason. Yet for all I knew they might have been chewing over my outstanding virtues, which are lacking in others.

The fact is that it does take all sorts to make a world, or anyway, this world is made up of all sorts. But the majority are not extremes. There are small people and big people, but relatively few dwarfs or giants. There are quiet people and not-so-quiet people, introverts and extroverts and so on.

This preamble was to make it quite clear that in introducing Jane into my speech with "It takes all sorts to make a world," it isn't meant as any kind of apology.

I describe Jane as a quiet person. She wouldn't disagree with that. It's no measure of her worth any more than if she were fat or thin. Only if she were fat, there'd just be more of her, that's all.

Now, why I'm at pains to point this out is because in some people's minds, a quiet person is slightly inadequate — simply because they don't "come over" as much as others. It's a totally false impression.

Empty vessels make the most sound, and the converse follows logically — "Full vessels make the least sound." "Still waters run deep" is another way of illustrating the same thing.

If somebody natters incessantly, it's invariably small talk, because serious reflection on deep matters cannot take place if you're jabbering all the time. If Bertrand Russell had gossiped non-stop about the price of eggs and old Mrs. Whatsit's bad leg, he wouldn't have had time to do all that thinking.

Anyway, some people say, "Still waters run deep" enough as to say, as they do with a meaningful nod and wink, "It's always the quiet ones!"

It's not always the quiet ones, whatever it is. John isn't all that quiet, but it's him as well.

Jane and John have already been living together, as you will know, and this now familiar modern practice — well, modern to my generation — cuts across the full spectrum of society and of people. All sorts waive a marriage ceremony, in the short term or the long. What does separate the wheat from the chaff in this matter is the degree of responsibility with which this course of action is taken. There are the "couldn't care less" type who casually start living together without forethought, and there are those who enter into it only after much soul-searching. Needless to say, Jane and John are among the latter.

Mary and I are most happy with the outcome, and we rejoice that today begins a new relationship with the prospect of full family life.

Now to a different matter. Jane works in a bank and I expect that, like me, you've wondered what it's like to be "in the money" during your working day. How can people work calmly when they're dealing with gloriously thick wads of notes?

Well, it seems there's a conditioning course for all new trainees. There's a private room that they occupy for their first day. When they're shown in they see an enormous mound of loose five-pound and ten-pound notes. Naturally they throw themselves into the pile with a cry of ecstasy and grasp handfuls of notes, throwing them up into the air and screaming with delight.

After a full day of this, without thought of food or drink, they're carried, exhausted, out of the room. Having got it out of their system, they are no longer affected by huge sums of money.

Of course, the counter service at banks is far more organised and efficient today than it used to be. I can remember the time when it was a common complaint that if there were two girls behind the counter, they were sometimes too busy chatting to notice a customer's presence. In fact a senior had to step in once and say to a couple of girls engrossed in chat, "Look. *Do* attend to that customer. He's been pointing a gun at you for the past five minutes and pleading with you to put your hands up."

It's nice to know that Jane is a bank employee because of the security that goes with it. This is important when two people have ventured into the mortgage business together. Jane can feel that she'll be able to play her part in bolstering the family income and hopefully avoid the strain that less fortunate couples fall victim to.

Jane and John have made a sound start to their lives together and have laid down a solid foundation for marriage. They have, if you like, in modern parlance, got their act together before deciding that the time was ripe for marriage. I suspect that they wanted to ensure that the way ahead would not be an obstacle course before they committed themselves to making the marriage vow. Good luck to them.

John, you know that you are wholeheartedly welcomed into our family, and I am now going to ask everyone to join me in a toast to you and Jane.

Ladies and gentlemen, will you drink with me to the future happiness of Jane and John.

BRIDE'S FATHER No. 11

(Bride a nurse, groom a doctor)
(Relates to Best Man's speech no. 14, on page 152.)

First of all let me welcome everyone to this medical gathering. There are a few of us here who are not in the profession. If you're anything like me, you have a wonderful feeling of being in safe hands today. If any of you gentlemen would like to be rushed upon by nurses from all directions, all you have to do is pretend to choke on your piece of wedding cake.

Having said that, I trust that we don't have nurses racing in all directions to cope with an outbreak of choking turns.

Mary and I have enjoyed having medical expertise and help at hand in the shape of Jane, and very enlightening and reassuring it has been.

How pleased we were when we knew that Jane was entering the nursing profession! I think it's a feather in any girl's cap when she makes that decision. She's following in a long line of young women who are prepared to dedicate themselves to the care of others, with all the demands that the work entails.

Other occupations involve hard work and endurance, but a nurse has to cope with the pressure of work and the tribulations of dealing with difficult patients and still keep calm and alert. If she allows things to get on top of her and she slips up, it can have regrettable human consequences. She is at the sharp end, the tough end, and if I may put it like this, the dirty end. To my mind "noble" is not too lofty a word to describe a nurse's vocation.

I may be wrong, but I find it difficult to think that there's such a type as an undedicated nurse. It seems a contradiction in terms. You have to be dedicated to pursue the job. Any parent should be proud to have a daughter following the career, and Mary and I are no exceptions.

Now, after praise like that, if I choke on the wedding cake, I'll be the centre of the biggest rush of all.

John has been sitting listening patiently to that and I half expected him to pipe up with, "What about the doctors!" Well, it goes without saying that they, too, deserve the highest regard, but my function as the bride's father was to concentrate on Jane. What better way of pointing people in the right direction to view her worth than via her vocation?

If I may continue that theme just a little more, I should like to say that in spite of the many trying days — and nights — that mark a nurse's life, Jane has never faltered in her positive attitude to the job. Often enough she came home and poured out all the troubles of a bad day, but never have Mary and I detected any wavering of resolution to press on. The bellyaching, if Jane doesn't mind me calling it that (after all, bellyache is a medical matter), has never been anything more than the therapy of letting off steam. It was not discontent.

I hope that I, who am not directly involved, have not painted a harsh picture of nursing. My emphasis on its demands was to demonstrate the quality of person required to cope with those demands. The satisfaction derived from the performance of the duties makes it all worthwhile to those who undertake it with a will.

John, be prepared for your flattery now, as a doctor.

In a way a doctor is always "on call", because a medical emergency can arise at any time and anywhere that the doctor happens to be. He never knows when an immediate demand on his services will be made. He is never completely off duty.

If you were a plumber, for instance, settled comfortably in a theatre seat one evening after a day dealing with a burst water main, and something went wrong with the pipes backstage, you wouldn't know about it (unless the theatre was flooded and then you'd only be in the same boat as everyone else, if you could find one). But in the normal way nobody would come and confront the audience with, "Is there a plumber in the house?" You would know that you could relax and forget all about your work.

However, I seem to recall hearing that once during a show Groucho Marx came back onto the stage and said, "Is there a doctor in the house?" A man jumped up and said, "Yes. I'm a doctor." Groucho said, "How are you enjoying the show, doc?" You see, a doctor can't get away from it.

Doctor (SURNAME), may I formally welcome you into the family now that you and Jane are joined together.

To follow custom, I should offer you and Jane some advice on coping with marriage from my own experience. As it happens, "coping" is too strong a word. Marriage for Mary and me (well, for me, anyway) has not been something to be coped with. We've simply carried on as if we weren't married. I wonder if that's the advice I should offer. It's perhaps the wisest thing to disabuse your mind of the well-entrenched notion that married life is inevitably something of a problem.

Jane and John, you look after the health of other people. As part of your reward, you should have good health, and this is what we all wish you.

Ladies and gentlemen, would you join with me in drinking not only to the future health, but to the future happiness of Jane and John.

BRIDE'S FATHER No. 12
(Bride a junior school teacher)
(Relates to Bridegroom's speech no. 15, on page 110)

It seems to me that people enter the teaching profession from two different directions. In one direction lies the academic sphere. There are some people with an absorbing interest in a particular subject, who find it a congenial occupation teaching their speciality to others.

From the other direction come the people whose greater interest is in the young, and in their development. Speaking in general terms, the academic tends towards working with older children, where his academic bent comes into its own, whereas the other type is happy amongst younger ones.

This is, of course, the barest of generalisations. There is a great range between the extremes of these two, and many very academic types make a career of working with the youngest of children.

Jane was a "natural" for younger children, and this is where she can be bossy if she likes with impunity. She might get kicked now and again by an ill-tempered child, but in the main her size compared with that of her charges serves as an efficient deterrent.

It's gratifying for Mary and myself to know that Jane works amongst the children that she loves. Her constant daily practice in managing little ones will stand her in good stead in her own family future, not that we anticipate her having thirty children all about the same age.

That reminds me of a young lady teacher in a railway carriage who was fairly certain that she recognised the man sitting opposite as the parent of a child in her class. She said to him, "Excuse me, but aren't you the father of one of my children?" ... He said, "No, but can I put my name down?"

Ambiguities constantly cause misunderstandings in children's minds. A minor example is that of the little boy who was asked in a mental arithmetic session, "What's nine times nineteen?" He said, "A hundred and seventy-one." The teacher said, "Very good!" The boy said, "What do you mean — 'very good'? It's perfect."

Then there was the occasion — and this is quite true — when a class was told to draw a picture of the Garden of Eden. One little lad had made a quite authentic depiction, but the teacher was puzzled to see a motor car in it. She didn't want to sound critical, so she simply said, "I recognise Adam and Eve in the back of the car, but who is it in the front?" He said, "That's God driving them out."

Another true anecdote (although a name has been changed to protect the innocent) concerns the little girl with a playmate called Robin. She said to her mummy, "Me and Robin were lucky. We had 'secs' at school again today." Her mummy said, "*What* did you say?" She said, "Me and Robin had 'secs' again at dinner time." Her horrified mummy said, "What do you mean — 'sex'?" The little girl said, "You know — 'seconds.' If there's any dinner or pudding left over, some of us get a second helping."

John, you will already have heard from Jane quite a few titbits thrown up in the course of a day amongst the very young. Mary and I used to enjoy an almost daily ration of these, and you can look forward to them as a constant source of amusement. It will compensate for irksome little things that happen when Jane forgets that she's not amongst the children, and you get a clip round the ear for mislaying your pen.

Come what may, John, Mary and I have great pleasure in welcoming you into our family.

As far as any advice goes that I can offer to you both, Jane and John, in your married state, perhaps I should follow up what I've said about Jane forgetting that she's not at school, when she's with you, John. Jane, John's a big boy now. Don't embarrass him in front of guests that you have to dinner by correcting the way he uses his knife and fork.

John, for your part, to keep the harmony play safe and do such things as standing up and saying, "Good morning, Miss" at the start of each day.

Remember that what pleases one partner can displease the

other, and you each have to accept displeasure as well as having pleasure.

For instance, when a couple arrived home one evening, their son said to his mother, "Grandma rang. Which do you want first, the good news or the bad news?" His mother said, "The good." The lad said, "Gran says yes, she *would* like to come and stay with us again." The mother said, "And the bad?" He said, "But only for two days."

Then he went out to his dad, who was putting the car away, and said, "Grandma rang. Which do you want first, the good news or the bad news?" His dad said, "The bad." The lad said, "Gran says yes, she *would* like to come and stay with us again." His dad said, "And the good?" He said, "But only for two days."

Ladies and gentlemen, I should like to propose a toast to our happy couple for their continuing happiness.

Would you raise your glasses please, and drink to the health and happiness of Jane and John.

PART 3
OTHER OPENING SPEECHES

OTHER OPENING SPEECHES No. 1
Bride's uncle

First of all I must say how sorry I am that Frank cannot be here today to deliver a speech as Jane's father. I know that the whole family share my regret at that. I felt something of an imposter when I stood at the front in church to give the bride away. There are two people who I imagine feel this regret far more keenly than any of us. The one is Frank himself and the other is Jane, who has been kind enough to brush the matter aside within my hearing, to save me feeling uncomfortable.

One thing we should bear in mind is that Frank would not want his absence to spoil Jane's special day. He wants us to be happy today, so we owe it to him to make a go of it.

If I am to be honest, once I was adjusted to the fact that Frank would sadly not be taking his rightful place today, it did give me a twinge of pleasure when I was invited to stand in for him. I have been given quite undeservedly a pleasure that it had never entered my head that I might have.

Jane has been a dear niece. I remember seeing her for the first time when she was only a day or two old. Since then she has grown into my affection. It isn't hard for anyone to see why. I know all brides are radiant on their wedding day, but Jane is always radiant. What a person is shines out of them, and "shine" is the appropriate word in the case of people like Jane.

Although I was touched at being asked to take Frank's place, when I attempted to prepare a speech in which to do justice to Jane, I found myself at a loss. That doesn't at all suggest that Jane is a loser. Far from it. It's a reflection on my ability as a speechmaker.

You could say to nearly everybody, "Write a speech about Winston Churchill", and they couldn't. They would quite literally be speechless. Now I could reel off a long list of Jane's virtues that have made her popular all along the line with friends, schoolmates, teachers, Brownie Brown Owls, Girl Guide leaders, Boy Scouts, Scoutmasters, soldiers, sailors, airmen ... sorry, Jane ... employers and so on. However, I'm stumped when it comes to composing a speech. Frank, in those time-honoured words written on a postcard, wish you were here.

If only I knew of a skeleton in Jane's cupboard, I'd have something to get my tongue round. There's Jane up there on her pedestal, shining with the glory of innocence, and all I can do is point to her. I'll have to content myself with doing that.

I've used the word "innocence", but there's a bit of a trick there, and it gives us a clue to what I want to say in my clumsy fashion about Jane. The glory that Jane shines with isn't innocence alone, because innocence is too negative to shine. Innocence only means absence of guilt. Given that we all fall from grace in small ways every day of our lives, we usually mean by an innocent person that they are free from serious fault. That is a way of life that is fairly easy. There's no great virtue in it, unless, of course, they have specific anti-social tendencies that require effort to keep in check.

It's empty praise to say of someone whose life has just ended, "He was a grand chap. He never did anybody any harm." The question is, "Did he do them any good?"

This is where Jane is not found wanting. She's a "do-gooder" − in the best sense, not the contemptuous sense in which the phrase has come to be used. She is one of those "help your neighbour" type who can make some of us feel a bit ashamed of ourselves for not doing more in that direction. Jane's energies are channelled into worthy causes. She's forever joining forces with groups organised to give help to those in need.

I hope this doesn't sound too much like preaching. It's only my way of banging Jane's drum − or blowing her trumpet. I don't think she's got a drum. Frank took one off her when she was little because he was worried about his own drum − his eardrum.

Right, enough about Jane's virtues. I was only pulling your legs. Now I'll tell you about all her vices. (LOOK AT WRIST WATCH) Blow! I shan't have time. I haven't even started on John yet.

Don't think I'd forgotten you, John. As a matter of fact, not knowing much about you first-hand, I made enquiries — at your local police station. I thought that would be a good place to start. Unfortunately they knew nothing about you. At my next attempt everything I heard about you was good. I realise now that it's too late, that I should have approached someone else besides your mother.

I did glean something from Ken. I got at him because you and he were old friends. It was very little, though. He said that as best man he would be making a speech himself after mine and naturally discussing you, and if he told me the juicy stuff about you, I would be queering his pitch.

Whatever he says, John, it's only going to be about your past, and at this moment our real interest is in your future. Every picture tells a story — and that means a true story. The picture of you and Jane together today has told of a fine young couple in tender harmony. Nothing could promise your future happy partnership better than that, and we are now going to drink to your future.

Ladies and gentlemen, I propose the toast to the health and happiness of Jane and John.

OTHER OPENING SPEECHES No. 2

Bride's grandfather

I never imagined that the pleasure of making a speech at Jane's wedding would fall to me. It wouldn't have happened if my little lad hadn't insisted and persisted and every other "isted" to get me to do this in place of him, because he was convinced that I could make a better job of it than he could. That was his way of saying, "Neither of us could make a decent speech but I'd rather you be in the hot spot than me."

He wanted to get out of people saying, "I didn't think much of Frank's speech, did you?" He'd much prefer them to say, "Didn't old Syd ramble on with a lot of drivel! It's a pity Frank didn't do the speech instead."

Now you'll know where the blame lies if you have to listen to rambling drivel for the next few minutes. It'll be Frank's fault.

John, before I go any further, one thing that I'm conscious of is that I referred to this occasion as Jane's wedding. Now, Jane couldn't get married on her own. There has to be somebody else getting married at the same time.

(BACK TO GUESTS) What I want to emphasise to John and all of you good folks is that I'm not speaking here as an oddbod. I'm speaking in place of the bride's father. As such I shall be talking far more about Jane than John. (TO JOHN) Anyway, as you are aware, John, you and I have had very little chance to get to know each other yet. Most of what I know about you is only hearsay. Don't you worry about that though, because I do know the truth about one thing. You can't believe all you hear.

What I do rely on, John, is Jane's evaluation of you. It's true that love is blind, but if you were other than the presentable young man that you appear to anyone, then the love wouldn't have been there in the first place. Jane is too shrewd. She gets it from her grandfather.

(BACK TO GUESTS) This is a proud day for the wife and myself as well as for Jane's mum and dad. It's gratifying for us to see our family flourishing. It was difficult enough for us to believe that we were grandparents — time flies so quickly — and now here we are already seeing the baby girl that made us grandparents herself grown up and married. We are both hale and hearty enough to be able to hope that we shall see a great-grandchild. If it's a little girl, then my dearest wish is that when she gets married, it's her granddad who's made to do a speech.

Having been in the wedded state for most of my long life, I am in a position to offer our newlyweds some timely advice. After the euphoria of the early days of marriage the tendency is for the couple to slip imperceptibly into a negative attitude of taking each other for granted. I read a letter to some newspaper or magazine in which a woman complained about husbands taking this attitude. She pointed out that when a man is welcoming a stranger into the house, he often makes the introduction to his wife with the words, "This is the wife."

The writer objected to the use of "the" before "wife". She said it gave away the husband's view of his wife as just another piece of furniture. It was like saying, "This is the table, this is the settee, this is the television set and this is the wife." A man wrote back and said that the woman who was complaining had misinterpreted the sense in which the word "the" was used. He said that what a man meant was "This is *the* wife" — which I thought was quite clever of him.

But to illustrate why a man should never take his wife for granted, there was a bullying type of husband whose wife was weak and submissive. She suffered in silence, bearing in mind her promise to love, honour and obey and so on "till death us do part". And this is exactly what she did — right up to the moment she shot him.

Now, it's a commonplace that there has to be "give and take" in marriage ... but how much trouble and misery could be avoided if only this were put into practice in its wider meaning! "Giving" doesn't simply mean a man saying to himself, "I suppose I'd better take the old cow a bunch of flowers for once, otherwise she'll start moaning — or mooing." It goes deeper than that.

However, ladies and gentlemen, I think I'll have to continue my offerings of advice to the newlyweds in private instead of taking up any more of your time.

May I now propose the toast to our two fine young people. Would you please join me in wishing them a happy future. Here's to Jane and John.

OTHER OPENING SPEECHES No. 3
Bride's brother

When it was first put to me that I should be the one to give Jane away at her wedding and make a speech, I was quite moved. It was as if suddenly all the threads that had bound us together as big brother and little sister had been pulled together.

It's perhaps when something like that happens that it's brought home to you what a person really means to you. Me having the honour of taking the place of the father at Jane's wedding! How thrilled I was! I must have felt more proud than most fathers do.

Until the subject was broached I hadn't really given much thought to who would take the father's place. I vaguely imagined someone in the older generation doing it. The idea of myself playing the role in a momentous occasion in Jane's life opened floodgates in my mind. I was overcome by nostalgic feelings of the affection that had characterised our brother-sister relationship since Jane was a toddler.

To be truthful I have to say a late toddler. In her early toddling days, to me she was ... (TO JANE) Cover your ears up, Jane ... just for a moment ... she was more of a nuisance than anything else.

That might sound unkind, but at that time I was a wretched little boy who chafed at having to look after little sister. The novelty of her advent into the family had worn off and it was only her nuisance value that I appreciated. I wasn't old enough to feel older-brotherly love. That was to develop later. Until then it fell to me to tie things up for her, loosen other things, disentangle her, reassure her that frogs don't bite and all that kind of thing.

As Jane became more capable of looking after herself and I became more reliable, we entered a stage of more general baby-sitting. This was when the first unconscious stirrings of affection for her must have taken place. When I say unconscious that isn't perhaps correct. It was more a matter of inability to recognise and identify those emotions in my own formative years.

My memory of Jane then is of someone who, for no reason other than that I happened to be around, had affection for me. She demonstrated that affection and this softened me up.

Now, Jane, here we are — you, that little girl, now a lovely bride, hearing things from your brother that you've never heard before. Isn't it strange that we can pour out our feelings about someone in their presence in public, even though we wouldn't do so in private! It all has to wait for an occasion like this.

I myself have been fled the nest for a while, and come to think of it, had I not been, there would have been a touch of sadness for me today at seeing you leave it. This is where I sympathise with Mum, but I won't dwell on that for the obvious reason. I myself should have sought comfort in the thought that I was not losing a sister, but gaining a brother.

It is indeed a great consolation to Mum that your partner is somebody like John. No, not somebody like John, but John himself. I don't suppose there is anybody like John. People have said to me, "I've never met anybody like John before!" They say it in a confidential whisper and with a worried frown. (TO JOHN) I don't know why they do that John, but at least it would seem that you are probably unique!

(BACK TO GUESTS) I suppose that just as we tend to take our parents for granted, we can do the same with our brothers and sisters. I know I took Jane with her sweet nature for granted. What if her nature had been sour instead? Quite seriously, the difference it would have meant to my life is beyond my conception. A sour sister! At least the alliteration imparts a ring to it. What about "The Sour Sisters"? It could be a pub run by two women.

It does make you think though, doesn't it? The good things in our life are easily overlooked, and the bad things we moan about. "Count your blessings" is sound advice. To count them all, and to appreciate how great some of them are, you have to stop and think, not merely say a few things off the top of your head. Having to prepare for this speech made me stop and think about Jane more than ever before, and I would just like to thank her for being such a great sister.

It goes without saying what a valued and loved daughter she has been as well. That's true, isn't it, Mum? (BACK TO GUESTS) If Mum had been doing a speech instead of me, you would have heard glowing praise for Jane as a daughter.

John, in view of what I've said about Jane, and about Mother and I being so happy that it's you that she's marrying, think what a compliment that is to you. If you'd heard these utterances before the wedding, you'd have needed to hire a larger size top hat.

Yes, John, you will find that being Jane's husband, the honeymoon will never be over. You're lucky. Some married men have told me that theirs never began.

You already know how welcome you are as a bright new star in the constellation which is Jane's family. On behalf of that family, I extend an enthusiastic welcome to your family as part of ours.

(BACK TO GUESTS) Now that I've said my piece, I expect Jane's ears are burning. It's time that I rounded off by giving you a chance to wet your whistles. I'm going to ask you if you would take your glasses, please, and join me in the traditional toast.

Ladies and gentlemen, I give you the toast to the health and happiness of Jane and John.

OTHER OPENING SPEECHES No. 4
Bride's uncle

There's something I should like to get straight first of all. Some of you will be wondering why Ken has called upon me to speak before Jane's dad does. The reason is that Jane's dad isn't going to speak ... I was pausing because I thought there'd be shouts of "Hooray!"

In fact (and you've got me worried now in case there are boos), I am speaking in his place. (GO TO PUT FINGERS IN EARS, GRIMACING IN ANTICIPATION OF BOOING) Right, now we know where we stand. At least, I know where I'm standing.

Now, the substitution was Frank's own doing. He asked me to stand in for him because I have the gift of the gab, as he elegantly phrases it, and he hasn't.

Initially I declined, on the grounds that an amateur speech from a father was better than a professional speech from an uncle. Modesty compels me to point out that I use the word "professional" very loosely.

However, Frank dug his heels in. It's what he used to do when we were kids, and by jumbo, does it hurt! The soreness still hasn't worn off!

He confessed that he was scared of messing up the delivery of what he wanted to say, and his appeal to me changed to a threat. He said that if I wouldn't do it, and it was left to him, he'd tell you some of the things that I got up to when we were young that would show me in my true colours. That's why it's me talking to you now, instead of Frank.

So to the substance of his message. There are two women in his life, and lovely they are, but my remarks concern today's star attraction, Jane. Now, John's people mustn't be offended at that description being applied to Jane singly. The bride always is the centre of attraction at any wedding. If John had been wearing the wedding dress, then *he* would have been the centre of attraction.

In John's own eyes, more than anybody else's today, Jane must be the star. Am I right, John?

(BACK TO GUESTS) What her dad wants you to know — and especially Jane herself — is that she has been a star attraction for him all her life, and not merely on special occasions, when she's been the belle of the ball, but also as Cinderella working in the kitchen. She's been everything to him that a daughter could be. She has been, and always will be, Daddy's little girl.

Jane has been a willing helpmate to her dad, whatever job he was doing, and his heart has been gladdened by the knowledge that she loved his company ... You know, I think he was too shy to say all this himself.

She delighted in doing things for him, and when there was nothing else that could be done, she'd make him a cup of tea. She'd do that on the slightest pretext. She'd make him tea when he arrived home from work, she'd make him tea if he looked a bit tired, she'd make him tea when he'd backed a slow horse, she'd make him tea when he wanted coffee ... You see that stomach of his? It isn't beer, it's tea. Out of the racing season, it goes down.

Have I got the message across all right, Frank?

You might attribute Frank's lavish parental praise to natural prejudice, but you'd be wrong. I can vouch for the truth of these words that he's said without moving his lips. I can bear witness to the quality of this father-daughter relationship. What I have conveyed to you from Frank is the sort of thing you would have heard had I been speaking to you as from myself.

There's something else that I know from first hand that Frank failed to mention. Jane's devotion is not confined to him. If Mary had been speaking today, she would be singing Jane's praises from the mother's viewpoint.

If there was an acknowledgement that a bride's father left out of his speech, he'd catch out from her mother. If I overlook one, I stand to catch out from her father as well as her mother, so let me get the acknowledgements made.

Frank and Mary extend their thanks to everyone who has helped towards the wedding, and there's a very special "thank you" to me for standing in for Frank.

Finally, on Frank and Mary's behalf, I now propose the toast to the bride and groom.

OTHER OPENING SPEECHES No. 5

Bride's brother
(father deceased)

It's been a particularly gratifying experience for me to take such an important place in Jane's wedding. I've had to be a bit of a father to her for some time past, but if I never quite felt the part before, I do now. To me, it's as if I were father more than brother. Taking Dad's place in Jane's life in various ways is nothing new to me, but this is a crowning event.

Naturally, there have been times when Jane has erred in her ways, and I have taken it upon myself to try and lay down the law with all the authority that I could muster. I've summoned her to my presence and, pacing up and down with hands clasped behind my back, I've lectured her sternly on the folly of consorting with young men unchaperoned. Jane stood there shaking — with laughter.

Well, it goes without saying that Mum has borne the brunt of our situation since we lost Dad, and it is she who has cared for us. Dad's death drew us all three closer together in mutual comfort and support. That slightly fatherly relationship that I've had with Jane is beginning to make me feel a wrench now that she's breaking away.

John, she's all yours now. If she gives you the happiness that she's given to Mum and me, then you are to be envied. Just remember that if Jane does stay out late with young men, it will be no use remonstrating with her. She won't take it seriously.

It's my pleasure now formally to propose the toast to you and Jane, with Mum's loving wishes and mine for your good fortune.

Ladies and gentlemen, would you please join me in drinking to the future happiness of Jane and John.

OTHER OPENING SPEECHES No. 6

Bride's grandfather
(father ill)

It's difficult for me to say that it's a pleasure to make this speech. Frank's unfortunate illness has deprived him of his joyful privilege. What a pity! How proud he would have been, escorting Jane to the altar! It's just one of those quirks of fate that we have to accept, but our sympathies are with Frank and Mary and Jane in their disappointment.

It's a case of "on with the motley". The last thing Frank wants is for the event to be overshadowed. On behalf of all of us I send out thoughts to him for a speedy recovery. He'll naturally be visualising what's going on here and be with us in spirit. I urge Jane especially to bear this in mind, so that her heart will be lighter about her Dad's physical absence.

In the short time that's been available to me to prepare an address in Frank's place, I've tried to conjecture what he might have said about Jane, and also what he wouldn't say.

Let me explain what I mean by that last bit before you get the wrong idea. When someone is very close to you, it can be a matter of not seeing the wood for the trees. A salient aspect of their character comes to be taken so much for granted that you lose conscious sight of it.

I suspect something about Jane that her dad would have overlooked because, to use a different metaphor, it was too much under his nose.

It's common enough to hear a person described as being of a bright and cheery disposition. Thank goodness that there is a generous scattering of such people, because they cheer us up by the briefest of encounters.

Now, Jane is one of that kind, but something more. She looks on the bright side of things. Not all cheery types do that. They can say, quite cheerfully, "Things will go on getting worse. The country's going to the dogs. When the world gets warmer, the sea will rise higher than inflation." They say it laughingly, but they believe it. They look on the black side. Their high spirits can cheer us, but their outlook can slightly depress us, mistaken though we know it is to see only bad in the future.

Every cloud has a silver lining. It's an ill wind that blows nobody any good, or as Shakespeare put it, "Sweet are the uses of adversity."

I remember one sunny day in Spring when there was a prolonged shower. There was a job that my brother and I wanted to do in the garden that required the ground to be dry. My brother said, "Don't worry. The rain's drying up as fast as it's coming down." I said, "The trouble is, it's coming down as fast as it's drying up."

That illustrates the two directly opposite ways of looking at the same thing.

We can, furthermore, be quite simply mistaken in our view of a situation, like the chap who was called up for the army during the war. He said to them, "It's no good you having me. I have one leg shorter than the other." They said, "That's all right. The ground where you're going's uneven."

I've tried to point out that being a jolly person and looking on the bright side do not have to go hand in hand. A quiet person can still be one who looks on the bright side. But when the two are combined, and combined in such a lovely girl as Jane, what a delight we have!

John, if you've been listening carefully, perhaps you'll have appreciated something more about Jane's worth. You can go round boasting, "My wife's not only jolly. She looks on the bright side of things." People will probably look at you and wonder which comedian it is that you're taking off.

Incidentally, John, I'd hate you or your people to get the idea that you're considered of small importance in the scheme of things. I've naturally spoken at length about Jane (well, I think I've only said one thing, but I know I've gone on a lot!) because that's what her father would have been expected to do. I could go on and on about her. In fact, a lot of people do go on about her, but that's another matter.

I know you more by reputation than the pleasure of personal contact, John. Happily, now that you're permanently installed in our family there'll be more scope for that pleasure. There's one warning I must give you, though. You've a high reputation to live up to.

I'd like to encompass everybody in my final words, because somebody's just held up a board saying, "ONE MINUTE". You and yours, John, are gladly welcomed into Jane's family, and Frank and Mary want everyone present to be thanked for taking part in this celebration.

I would ask you all now to join me, please, in the toast to the happy couple, Jane and John.

OTHER OPENING SPEECHES No. 7

Bride's uncle
(father deserted, couple already living together)

I've been looking forward to doing this speech because it does give me the opportunity to put you all in the picture about Jane and John.

As Jane's uncle I've been an intimate observer of the family scene, ever since her father unfortunately took his leave. I'm Jane's maternal uncle. I suppose that's how I'd be described. In other words I'm her mother's brother. However, I don't like the thought of being called a *maternal* uncle. It makes me sound effeminate. You might imagine me bottling the fruit. I feel *p*aternal, not *m*aternal, towards Jane. So if I want to be correct and give the whole truth, I can say that I'm her paternal maternal uncle.

It was when her dad left and I naturally took a sympathetic interest in the welfare of my sister and her daughter, that I grew closer to Jane, trying to do what little I could as something of a non-resident substitute father.

This closer contact gave me a better insight into Jane's character. Much of what I learned, although I didn't realise it at the time, was common to all girls. One thing I found out was that they liked young men.

I would have lent what support I could if only for Mary's sake, even if Jane had been a right young ... blackguard. I don't know whether girls can be blackguards, but the more female equivalent that came to my mind would not have found favour in a wedding speech. The fact that Jane was far from being a right young whatsit made it a pleasure to me to be involved.

In due course a particular one of those young men came on the scene. I think he's here today. (LOOK ROUND UNTIL EYES REST ON JOHN) Yes, here he is. I thought we couldn't keep him out of Jane's wedding. With some of his predecessors it was a case of "here today and gone tomorrow", but this one is more like "here today and here to stay".

When John had got his feet under the table he began to relieve me of some of my attendance upon Jane and her mother. However, the time came when Jane and John wanted to set up a home together, and as a result this happy event is now taking place. Both Jane's mum and I are very pleased that they are now permanently together in a stable and secure relationship.

Now, what advice can I give you both about marriage? You've experienced the married state for quite a while now, and you don't look any the worse for it, but at present there are only the two of you, and that has a habit of changing ... (GLANCE AT JOHN) I believe John's getting the wind up because he's visualising Jane's mum and me and others all moving in with them.

(TO JOHN) No, what I have in mind is not that, but it is something that will entail you and Jane sharing the task of getting the wind up.

Life involves learning by mistakes. But where possible learn by the mistakes of others. That way you get your lessons free.

Proper communication between husband and wife is important. Remember that managing a large family can impose a strain on your relationship at times. A woman was looking down the back garden once and she said to her husband, "I'd love some orchids." He nearly had a fit. He thought she said, "I'd love some *more* kids."

Anyway, it's high time that I let you all finish what you were saying to each other when you were stopped in order to listen to me.

I ask you now to drink a toast to the continuing health and happiness of Jane and John.

OTHER OPENING SPEECHES No. 8

Bride's uncle
*(parents divorced and not present, bride fostered by uncle
and aunt)*

I expect that everyone who has been kind enough to accept an invitation to this happy event is aware of the family situation. My wife and I have had the privilege and joy of being guardians to Jane for many years, my wife being Jane's aunt.

When I escorted Jane up the aisle today it was with great pride and joy. To my wife and me she will always be as a daughter.

The one way that we fell short as parents in the early stages was that we tended to spoil our charge. That was because we were eager to make up to her for having been cheated out of a happy life with her own parents. Looking back, we see that we could have done Jane a great injustice if our treatment of her in that way had succeeded. It is to her credit that she was resistant to being spoiled.

In fact, Jane was more of a positive influence on us. She licked us into shape as parents. She sensed where to draw the line and prevent us from being overindulgent with her. She also had to get the message across that she wasn't the helpless little girl that we were treating her as.

As Jane blossomed into a fully-fledged teenager, she was introducing us to the outside world. This wasn't the world that we lived in. We fondly imagined that we were *au fait* with modern society, but we didn't know the half of it. We began to feel that Jane had adopted us, instead of the other way about, and that she was bringing us up.

Jane, you have kindly intimated to us time and again your gratitude for taking you on board, as it were. Now Mary and I have the intense pleasure of making it known to all family and friends here that we are endlessly grateful to you for what you have given us in return.

I used the nautical expression "on board", and when you'd had time to look around you must have thought that our ship was "Noah's Ark". It wasn't that there were courting couples of giraffes and whatnot about, but the general atmosphere of being behind the times. I suppose you thought I was Noah. I wonder if that was why, when we were discussing a name for the house, you suggested "The Ark".

I think it was the little things that gave us away, like when you were doing a crossword and one of the clues was "a modern dance" in six letters and I said, "The veleta". Then there was the time that a canvasser called, trying to get us to modernise our lighting — and I said we weren't going to squander money like that. We'd stick to gas.

To my wife and me Jane came as a breath of fresh air, and she has continued to blow through our lives as such. When she announced her engagement to John we could only be delighted.

John, you already know the extent of your welcome into such family as Jane possesses. Because my wife and I look on Jane as a daughter, we ask the favour of looking on you as a son.

The bride's father — or his substitute — usually trots out some advice on marriage in his speech, but with your common sense and Jane's, I can't think of anything at this stage that wouldn't be superfluous, so I'll waive the tradition.

It is with the greatest of pleasure, and perhaps tears in my eyes, that I propose the toast to the welfare of our bride and groom.

Would you all rise, please, and drink with me to the future health and happiness of Jane and John.

PART 4
BRIDEGROOM'S SPEECHES

BRIDEGROOM No. 1

Most couples on their wedding day describe it as the happiest day of their lives. That worries me. It implies that as from tomorrow there's a lifelong decline ahead, so I'm making the most of today. However, I must say that today is so happy that even days less happy could still be blissfully happy ones. All those of you with an 'A' level in logic will be able to follow that.

I should like to stress the gratitude that Jane and I feel towards you for being here. I've been a guest at many a wedding, and when I've heard one of the hosts say to the guests, "Thank you all for coming," I've thought what a touching, undeserved courtesy it is, because it is we, the guests, who owe all the thanks for being invited. Now, however, for the first time I know what it's like to be the bridegroom, and I can understand that what prompts that expression of thanks is more than courtesy. It's the guests that create the party atmosphere, and you good people have certainly done that for Jane and me.

I'm sure that my dear wife, as I am now proud to call her, feels the same ... (TO JANE, NASTILY) Don't you! Well, speak out! I'm your husband — you're supposed to back me up! (BACK TO GUESTS) I suppose I'll have to be patient and give her a few more hours to get used to the new order of things.

As I was saying before I was so rudely uninterrupted, my wife and I thank you sincerely for your presence, and we thank you also for your presents. Your presence is a joy to us because it's this happy gathering that is making our day, and your delightful presents would be a joy to possess in themselves, but because of the unique occasion in our lives that they mark, they are going to be an even greater joy, and a lasting one.

On the subject of gratitude, there is something of which I have been increasingly aware ever since childhood, now being an opportunity to express this publicly, and that is a deep gratitude to my Mum and Dad for being such loving and caring parents.

These are not hollow words. I can never repay the debt that I owe them for all that they have done for me. The upbringing, the guidance, the support and comfort ... It's impossible, isn't it, to sum up adequately what golden parents have given you? One aspect that I should like to put the spotlight on because of the occasion is the example that they have set for me. Besides their loving devotion as parents, they have demonstrated an unfailing devotion to each other, and that is an example that shines brightly in my vision now, because I have just entered into the same state, that of marriage, in which they have set that example. The least I can do is to follow it.

(LOW VOICE IN SERIOUSNESS) What I promised formally in church, I repeat as I face you all. I will devote my life lovingly to the precious bride that I have so undeservedly gained today ... (SHARPLY TO JANE) Are you listening!

Of course that is one way that I can repay Jane's parents, not only for granting me the hand of their daughter, but for making me feel so at home with them and treating me like a son — in short, for welcoming me as a suitable partner for Jane.

Both Jane and I would like to thank her parents very much indeed for providing the wedding for us. Everything has been a delight, and we are most grateful.

There's someone whose assistance has been invaluable to me not merely today, but during the run-up, and that is, of course, my best man, Ken. I'm thankful that he allowed me to lean on him so heavily — as we came home from the stag party. I think if he hadn't turned up for the wedding, I shouldn't have either. He might not look like an angel, but he's been a guardian angel to me all along the line. Thank you, Ken.

Before I reseat myself, there's a very pleasant duty that I have to perform, and that is to propose a toast to the bridesmaids. Those young ladies are a delight to the eye. I don't know if there's a collective noun for bridesmaids, but I do know that we say "a bevy of beauties", and I think that therefore "a bevy of bridesmaids" sounds perfectly apt.

It's not only their appearance to which I pay tribute, but to the charming way in which they have taken part in today's ceremony, with their radiantly smiling faces. They graced the scene at the church, and they grace our gathering here.

So, it is, then, that in thanking all of you for making our day the joyful one that it is, and in wishing you enjoyment in the rest of the festivity, that I gladly ask you to stand and raise your glasses and drink a toast to our bonny bridesmaids.

BRIDEGROOM No. 2

First of all I should like to thank Jane's Dad for his kind words. Secondly I should like to get a dig at him for making such a good speech, because I'm having to follow it. Mine will undoubtedly suffer by comparison — and I myself am suffering enough at having to make a speech at all. I think if you asked elderly bachelors why they never married, many would reply that it was through fear of making a speech at the wedding reception.

Be that as it may, you can take it from me that whatever I do say springs from the heart and is not a clutching at platitudes. That's the trouble with platitudes. You may wish to express a feeling simply and sincerely and it comes out as a commonplace, with nothing to indicate the depth of feeling behind it, such as when I first said to Jane, "I love you". That's why I've never bothered to say it to her again.

Anyway, actions speak louder than words and I've had time to prove my love to her, otherwise I don't suppose that she would be sitting where she is today — or if she were sitting there, I wouldn't be standing here. There'd be a different lucky man standing in my place.

I should like to thank all of you, on behalf of Jane and myself, simply for being here on our great day. You all look very happy, apart from George there, but he never looks happy even when he is. I think that's the best way that you could have blessed our marriage. It's a wonderful feeling to look round and see our families and friends chatting freely together with such gaiety as though there were something good to celebrate, and I feel a little humbled by it, because it means that you approve of Jane and me being entrusted to each other's care. It's made me think to myself, "If I let Jane down in the future, I'd be letting all of these special people down," so you can see how valuable your presence is. Thank you, indeed.

Of course everyone who has been blessed with a happy home life recognises how fortunate he or she has been when they learn of the unhappiness of children in other circumstances, and they feel that they have received a priceless gift from their parents, something which is beyond reciprocation. They are quite right. I know, because I am one of those fortunate ones.

Now that I am married I feel there is a way to reciprocate, at least partly, even though that way is an indirect one, and that is by emulating my parents — well, one of them, because I can be a good father, even if I can't be a good mother. That's where Jane comes in. If I give to our offspring what my parents gave to me, they will surely be gratified to see their example bearing fruit.

During the time that Jane and I were engaged there was an episode when I was struck with anxiety about our future married state. It happened when I entered the lounge at Jane's. She was visibly startled and before she rose to greet me she hurriedly hid a book under the cushion where she was sitting. She looked very flustered, but I pretended not to notice anything unusual. As soon as she'd gone into the kitchen to make some tea, I whipped the cushion aside to see what the book was — and I was shocked ... It was called "How to boil an egg ". Can you imagine how I felt!

However, when I confronted Jane with it she assured me that the title was only a light-hearted one, and that egg boiling didn't occupy the book from cover to cover. There was more to it than that. I was greatly relieved to learn that not only could I look forward to a boiled egg from Jane, but bacon to go with it.

Now, Jane and I would like to convey our special thanks to Ken, my best man, for the flair with which he has discharged his duties — but don't think they're finished yet, Ken. May his best man be as good to him when his turn comes, as he has been to me. Without him I might have put the ring on the wrong finger, and found myself married to the vicar.

Jane joins me in thanking her parents heartily for providing this day for us. Thank you indeed, Mr. and Mrs. Jones.

Finally, I turn my attention gladly to those lovely young ladies, our bridesmaids. They have done us proud and attracted many an admiring glance. It seems a waste that they can't be bridesmaids a lot more often before they're snapped up as brides. Why not start a business — "Rent a bridesmaid"? Well at least we have had the pleasure of their gracious services and decorative presence.

Ladies and gentlemen, may I ask you to rise and join a toast to our unforgettable bridesmaids.

BRIDEGROOM No. 3

First of all, on behalf of Jane as well as myself, I should like to thank Mr. Jones for all the nice wishes for us that he's expressed. It was interesting for me listening to him, because I've learned a lot more about Jane than I ever knew before. It's given me food for thought. If I'm not mistaken there was a bit of gloating going on inside Jane's dad because he and her mum had succeeded in palming off their daughter onto an unsuspecting victim.

However, one has to take the good with the bad, the rough with the smooth, the ups with the downs, the ins with the outs and so on. From the good and smooth and ups and ins that I know about Jane they'll more than compensate for their opposites.

Fortune smiled on me the day that we met. I had a win on the pools. That reminds me of a conversation that I was in on where a young chap desperate to gain the hand of a certain young lady asked our older, long married acquaintance, "How did you win your bride?" He said, "In a raffle." The lovesick young one was taken back by this outright cynicism and the older man then looked down and said wistfully, "I wish I'd won the *first* prize. It was one pound fifty."

I dare say that in time to come I might trot that out about Jane, but something that I am sure of is that there will be no grain of cynicism in it. (TURN TO JANE IN SLIGHT ALARM) I assume your dad was joking in some of the things he said about you! (BACK TO GUESTS) Getting cold feet is something you're supposed to do *before* the wedding ceremony, not after it. My feet have started to feel chilly. I'll imagine Jane handing me my slippers that she's warmed by the fire when I've come in from clearing the snow away ... and taking the dog for a walk ... and doing the shopping ... and doing errands. I think there's another one to add to my "good and bad" list — taking the warm with the cold.

It's something for a bridegroom to be grateful for that his parents don't have to make a speech. It's bad enough knowing − or rather not knowing − what your best man's going to say to embarrass you. There's always the consolation that people don't believe the best man, because he's supposed to entertain the guests with a tissue of lies. Now that I've said that, I'm afraid Ken will abandon his prepared material and say all nice things about me and you won't believe them.

Before my thoughts stray, let me get my "thank you's" in, because they're important. Apart from the question mark over his coming speech, I'd like to thank Ken for the way he has carried out his best man offices. He has afforded me, for one, considerable amusement and I thank him heartily ... Well, we know a best man can get confused, because it's not something he does every day, but I mean, when the vicar asked, "Wilt thou have this man to thy wedded husband ...?" and Ken said, "Yes," I thought it was a bit much ... It's a good job it wasn't the first wedding that the vicar had ever conducted, otherwise he might have been thrown off course.

It's natural for a young person starting married life to think back over his or her past and to ask questions. This is a kind of watershed and the mind travels back nostalgically. It's not so much the more adult years when, like myself, you've set yourselves up in a flat, but the earlier part of your life when you were being brought up, as the expression goes.

Now, when I looked at myself in the mirror this morning when I was all set to start off for the church, I thought, "What a fine, upstanding young chap! Your parents did a good job with you!" That's why I want to congratulate Mum and Dad on the wonderful job that they did, and to thank them for it.

That sounds pathetically inadequate now that I've said it. It's only taken a few seconds. How can a few seconds cover seventeen or eighteen years? Well, if I went on for ten minutes the question would be, "How can ten minutes cover seventeen or eighteen years?" So let's leave it at that. Perhaps, hopefully, it will say as much as could be said in the brief time at my disposal.

I will simply say to Mum and Dad, "Thank you for

everything." Only they and I know what is contained in the word "everything".

I only hope that as the future unfolds, Jane and I don't have to deal with such an awkward cuss as I was. The saying, "Like father, like son" sends a chill down my spine.

My next bouquet of thanks goes to Jane's parents. Firstly, I'd like to thank them for having Jane, and secondly for letting me have her. I'm grateful to them for accepting me from the start, when Jane took me into their home and said, "Look what I've found."

Now I speak on behalf of Jane also, because we both want to thank you all for being here and for all your good wishes and indeed those exciting-looking gifts that we've only had time to glimpse at. I can't wait till the honeymoon's over so that we get back and look at them properly.

Jane and I wish to express our very real gratitude to her mum and dad for "giving" us this day. We thank them for their kindness in being unsparing to make our send-off so memorable.

A special thanks now to some special people today. What would a wedding be like without bridesmaids? Ours might not have been bridesmaids before, but they've conducted themselves with such poise that you wouldn't know it. When I say that they've decorated the church and this room I don't mean they used distemper and a brush.

What better note to end on than a toast to those young ladies, whom Jane and I thank heartily for being the icing on today's cake!

Ladies and gentlemen, would you join in that toast please. The bridesmaids.

BRIDEGROOM No. 4

(He has been a tearaway)

This is a day that I've been looking forward to with great delight — not because of the wedding, but because of this opportunity to get up and say what I think to the whole circle of my family and friends. It is something to relish because I've done it before. I was a best man and I revelled in the prospect of being able to say not so much what I thought, but what I didn't think. The best man can take the mickey out of the groom as much as he likes.

Come to think of it I might have been premature in my anticipation, because the boot could be on the other foot this time. I'm not in the happy position of being able to use somebody as an Aunt Sally, because the bridegroom's speech is constrained to moderate limits in that direction, but for all I know Ken might have a store of coconuts ready to throw at me.

What frustrates me is the order in which speeches are made. If I indulge in derogatory statements about Ken, he has the advantage of denying them and turning the tables on me when he makes his speech. I'm not allowed to make another speech after him, in which I could redress the balance.

Ladies and gentlemen, the best thing, I think, if you don't mind, is if you all put your hands over your ears throughout Ken's speech.

Now, I want to thank Jane's dad for his exposé of my future wife's ... I mean my present wife's ... well, my one and only wife's foibles. Some I'd already come across, but others were news to me. She must have been saving them up till we were married. One day I could open a drawer and find it full of foibles.

It's a bit disconcerting, isn't it, when only an hour or two after you've married somebody you start finding out a lot about them that you didn't already know. If I'd overheard Mr. Jones rehearsing his speech before the wedding, I might have called it off. It's not so much what he's told us that worries me as what he might have left out. My tearaway days are over.

I'll tell you about my misspent youth by way of thanking my parents for putting up with me. If it weren't for their dedication to the cause of saving me from myself I shouldn't be standing here now as an acceptable husband for Jane. It was their unflagging patience and perseverance that won out in the end and made me pull myself together. What a burden to them I must have been!

My rebelliousness started early in life. Mum and Dad worried when I stopped out so late. Mum would stand on the doorstep calling, "Johnny, where are you! It's past your bedtime!" Midnight is a bit late for a seven year-old, isn't it?

From then on it was downhill all the way. When I was sixteen I crept back into the house at one o'clock in the morning and Mum said, "What time do you call this! You should have been in bed two hours ago!" I said, "I was."

Night after night I arrived home the worse for drink and tried to hide it, like when I sat calmly looking at the newspaper until Dad pointed out that it was upside down, so I tried to stand on my head.

There isn't time, thank goodness, to tell you all the gory details. The important point is that Mum and Dad suffered me when they could easily have thrown me out in my late "teens". Instead they were determined to reform me, exhausting every form of persuasion and coercion. In the end it paid off. I don't think there's any need for me to labour the point any more.

Those wretched years are water under the bridge. Meeting Jane was timely. She helped me along my road to recovery. Her steadying influence should not be underestimated. She was something new in my life that gave me a sense of purpose and transformed me. From irresponsibility I was led into responsibility. It's not every ne'er-do-well that is lucky enough to have a Jane come into his life and join with him like this. I owe Jane as well as Mum and Dad a deep debt of gratitude.

Well, Ken, it might seem to our guests that I have pre-empted a good deal of what you were going to say about me. Now that I've come clean, I've probably ruined your speech. You were put on the spot really because as best man you're supposed to pile the agony on for the fun of things, and however bad the things were that you said they wouldn't have been far from the truth. You could have been embarrassed by your own speech. Just make up some nice things about me as you go along. Imagine that you're talking about yourself, then it shouldn't be too difficult. (BACK TO GUESTS) That can be taken two ways, can't it?

Now that I've unburdened myself about my disgraceful past I feel the need of a drink, so if you good people don't mind, I'll end my speech, but before I do so let me say that it's great to have you all here together.

I don't think I've yet thanked you from both of us for all your presents — and the good wishes that have come with them. In any case you'll be hearing from us about your gifts individually.

Not least we want to thank Jane's mum and dad for providing this wonderful day for us. It is not only your generosity, Mr. and Mrs. Jones, for which we are grateful, but the enthusiastic spirit with which you have organised things. Thank you so much.

There are people we wanted to thank for their help in the preparations for today. I apologise for my mental block — I'm sorry I can't just reel their names off, but your services are not undervalued, I can assure you. Jane and I will see you afterwards to thank you again in person.

There is one small group of people that I'm not forgetting to convey our thanks to, probably because their youthful glitter commands my attention. Thank you, dear bridesmaids, for the help that you have been at the service. You get ten out of ten for that, and ten out of ten for your delightful appearance. That's twenty out of ten altogether, and that can't be bad. You can still sit there looking pretty while the rest of us honour you with a toast.

Ladies and gentlemen, will you join me in raising our glasses to the bridesmaids.

BRIDEGROOM No. 5

(Brought up without a father)

Now that I'm leaving my mother's tender care and starting a new home life, I'd like to thank Mum *for* that tender care and for my upbringing.

After we lost Dad life was difficult for Mum with us lads to cope with, but cope with us she did, well and truly! If she wasn't either quelling a squabble or darning a pocket or trying to find school dinner money, she was doing all three at the same time.

Mum had to read the Riot Act to us so often that eventually she knew it off by heart.

If she has any reward, it's in seeing the fine, upstanding sons that we have become. Isn't that right, lads! In fact I'm so fine and upstanding that even such a sought-after young lady as Jane agreed to marry me .... even if she was blind drunk at the time.

Mum has at last acquired a daughter, and the odds are it won't be the only one. Jane has landed herself with an assortment of brothers that she didn't bargain for, but she's prepared to take the good with the bad .... I'm the good and they're the bad. (That's another two dozen tin cans tied on the back of the car.)

Mum's happy that I've married one of the "girl next door" kind. I know a middle-aged couple and the man told me that his was an instance of marrying the girl who actually lived next door .... He wishes she still did.

As we lads have got a bit older we've taken a share with the chores, because it was a lot for Mum, but life's going to be different for me now because Jane will only have the two of us to look after, so she should manage without any help from me.

I shall lie in bed on a Sunday morning studying the breakfast menu and give Jane my order as soon as she's back from her paper round. This is what's expected of the "girl next door" type, so Jane should take my expectations as a compliment.

If you want to determine fully what is meant by one description you should think about its opposite, with which you may be more familiar.

What is your image of a young woman the opposite of the "girl next door" type? You'll surely agree that she's not a home-loving, caring wife, but a self-seeking good-time girl who wants all she can get out of life and neglects her husband, whom she looks upon as somebody to provide for her, the more luxuriously the better.

She's the sort who wouldn't dream of waiting on her husband hand and foot — which I am sure Jane dreams of. She expects to be taken out for a meal on her birthday because she can't be bothered to cook 365 days of the year.

She thinks herself hard done by if she doesn't get a little surprise gift now and then, like a few flowers — as if her husband's got nothing better to do with his money than lash out in wasteful ways like that. He's got to skimp and save to keep taking his turn paying for rounds of drinks every evening, with his friends.

This is how selfish and thoughtless such a person is. Once the ring is on the finger they think they can put their feet up and take their ease, while the poor husband has to do everything from cleaning his own shoes to loading his golf clubs into the car, and fetch and carry for himself every time she's gone gadding off to the dentist's.

Anyway, I really must be brief now or else the plane will go without Jane and me for a start. I, personally, would like to thank Jane's parents for the way they've befriended Mum. I thank them as well for oiling the wheels for me and Jane. I don't mean on the wedding car, I mean for things like going out for a walk in a thunderstorm when I called round to see her.

What we both want to thank them for is providing the wedding itself. Things could not have been nicer. We really are appreciative of what you have done.

Jane and I want to thank everybody for the wonderful array of gifts. We would love to spend more time looking at them, but that will have to wait.

Ken, you must be singled out for a personal "thank you" from me in the way of help and support as my best man. You've done a lot behind the scenes. I just hope that that bridesmaid doesn't tell her mother.

That brings me to what Jane has asked me to do — to acknowledge how helpful those pretty young bridesmaids have been to her. We both thank you sincerely.

What better way for me to end than by proposing their health and happiness? Bridesmaids, prepare to be toasted. You all look very healthy and happy, but our wish is for that to continue.

So, ladies and gentlemen, I invite you to join me in expressing our appreciation of those young ladies. The bridesmaids!

BRIDEGROOM No. 6

More than one person has asked me how I was feeling about making today's speech. I had to confess to something akin to nervousness because it is something new to me. I've never given a bridegroom speech before. In fact I've never given a speech of this nature before. Brief addresses to meetings, yes, and I can't plead inexperience at public speaking up to a point, but this is a different matter.

You're all my family and friends, so why should I approach this performance with a touch of the whatsits? I'll tell you. It's the difference in importance between this and the other usual instances of speaking. You might think it would be the other way about — that addressing a gathering of people outside the circle of family and friends would be more likely to cause jitters than this free-and-easy occasion. No. Even though this is that kind of occasion, there are important things that I want to be sure to say and I'm afraid of overlooking them.

The point is that I've discussed with Jane the acknow-ledgements that we both want to make, and if I do forget any then not only shall I kick myself afterwards, but Jane might kick me as well. That's the sort of "oneness" that we already have, you see ... At least, if I do fall down on the job, I'll get a kick out of it.

Now, Jane, you thought you knew all the "thank you's" that were going into my speech, didn't you? Well, there's one you didn't know about, and that's coming first. I thank you, Jane, for becoming my lovely bride. You can't help being lovely, but you could help becoming my bride. In my preliminary notes I left a pause after that for anybody who wanted to go, "Oh, isn't that sweet!"

Those who didn't have that reaction probably consider it an odd thing for a groom to say publicly. Surely he could write himself a reminder to say it to his bride in private. But then why do we make acknowledgements publicly when we've already made them in private or intend to do so? It's because the thanking in public (that word doesn't sound right for us lot, but you know what I mean) not only adds weight to it, but by drawing everybody's attention to where thanks are due, it is hoped that the party on the receiving end better appreciates the sincerity of those thanks.

You might wonder why I should be grateful to Jane for marrying me. I suppose it's because I feel that I don't deserve her. (LOOK DOWN AT NOTES AND SAY "Pause for spontaneous outbursts of protest.") She's been a good influence on me already, and I feel I've become a better person for knowing her. She brings out the best in me. Perhaps if I hadn't become an improvement on what she first found, she wouldn't have married me.

Turning to my mum and dad, they've been kindness itself to me and my brothers and sisters. With such a mixed bunch as we turned out to be, it must have taxed their ingenuity to bring us all up, but they succeeded admirably. Thank you, Mum and Dad, for everything. There was always harmony between yourselves in the home and you worked as a team. That's something I know now with hindsight. It formed the basis for your success in dealing with us individually and keeping relations between us kids on an even keel. If you were to be paid in money for the years that you worked at that, you would be millionaires.

Talking about Jane influencing me for good, it's worth remembering that in marriage one partner often becomes like the other. I can't decide which would be better − Jane ending up bald and with a moustache, or myself flitting about in a dress ... It would confuse the kids. In fact, if it happened too soon, it's unlikely that there'd be any.

You do hear some frightening tales about married life though, don't you? Some men vow that they wouldn't venture into the dark unknown of matrimony, and warn others of the evils that wait in store for the unwary bridegroom. That reminds me, I haven't yet thanked you, Ken, for being so conscientious as my best man. Thank you also for your advice ever since you heard that I intended to wed. I hope I haven't offended you by not taking it.

(BACK TO GUESTS) Thank you, everyone, from Jane and me, for all your good wishes and gifts. They are both greatly appreciated. I don't mean both the gifts, I mean both the good wishes and the gifts.

Thank you also Mr. and Mrs. Jones, for the bountiful gift of the wedding itself. Jane and I are deeply grateful.

There's one more party for special mention. They're shining away in their glory like little glow-worms. They are reserved till last because I'm privileged to propose a toast to them after thanking them, as I do, for being our bridesmaids and for conducting themselves so beautifully.

Ladies and gentlemen, I should like to finish now on that note. Would you please stand and join me in the toast to the bridesmaids.

BRIDEGROOM No. 7

(Couple met through dating agency)

There's probably no-one here who isn't aware that Jane and I met through a dating agency. According to a computer we were likely to be suited. That's a laugh for a start. What does a computer understand about people's personalities?

That doesn't invalidate the service that the agencies provide. You see, when any strangers meet for the first time, it's the same situation. They may wish to meet again, but whatever exchange of information has taken place between them, and whatever glimpses they have had of each other's character at first encounter, all this is only superficial.

In a way Jane and I met by chance. We both happened to live in the same area and both happened to register with the same dating agency at around the same time.

When you use those places you can't get anything tailor-made. You have to accept what's going.

A man can go into a tailor's shop for a suit, and if they haven't one that fits him in the material he wants and he likes the look of, then they'll make him one up.

You can't order your ideal partner from a dating agency, but then neither can you from anywhere else. Dating agencies exist to bring two people together who are likely to hit it off. This is what our agency did, and today is the most enjoyable date we've yet had.

I don't know what Ken's got up his sleeve to say on the subject of how Jane and I met. I've talked to him in this vein before, and he might have been going to speak along the same lines. Sorry if I've sabotaged your speech, Ken.

Ken's been a good friend to me, by the way, and after giving the question of his suitability careful thought, I decided against applying to an agency for a best man.

It's been interesting for Jane and myself to discover how many things we have in common. It's made us try to recall the details about ourselves that we had given to the agency. But I'm sure that the computer didn't know that neither of us liked streaky bacon.

Of course being different doesn't mean being incompatible. Although actually Jane and I *are* incompatible. I've got the income and Jane is very pattable!

It's the discovery of the differences in temperament and your likes and dislikes that can be fun. Jane and I have found that, and the discoveries that have been made through experiences, rather than by telling each other, have given us some laughs when we've thought about it afterwards. That's one thing that it's important to have in common if you plan to marry — a sense of humour.

Well, enough about us, except that it's we who want to thank you all for your good wishes and gifts. You've given us a wonderful send-off to start our married life. Our respective families have rejoiced in our match and that has enhanced our happiness.

I should like to take this opportunity to thank my mum and dad not only for their interest and encouragement throughout the period of my meeting with and engagement to Jane, but for all that they have done for me and been to me. I am glad that I have been able to give them the happiness of seeing me married to Jane.

We both wish to express our gratitude to Jane's parents for providing the wedding. You have our sincere thanks.

For his special services I thank Ken, my valiant right-hand man, and Jane and I want to thank her little troupe of bridesmaids, whose appearance has lent a touch of magic to today's events.

It's a special pleasure for me to propose a toast to them. Ladies and gentlemen, would you please drink with me to the bridesmaids.

BRIDEGROOM No. 8

The last time I was at the V.I.P. table at a wedding was when I was a best man. I feel as though I've moved from the witness box to the dock ... I wonder if Jane will bring that remark up for the next fifty years? Every time we're having a row and throwing things at each other, she'd throw that at me as well. What a price to pay for one thoughtless moment!

Ah, well!

"The moving finger writes; and, having writ,
Moves on: nor all my piety nor wit
Shall lure it back to cancel half a line,
Nor all my tears wash out a word of it."

Or, if you like, "What's done is done, and cannot be undone."

Am I forgiven, Jane? When I said, "in the dock," it was only my tactless way of saying that my speech would be taken more seriously than in my previous role, and I should have to choose my words. I've blundered at the start. Can I go out and come back in again?

(BACK TO GUESTS) There must be many a man who's made a mess of his marriage, and wished he could go out and come back in again. I don't intend to be as clumsy as that. I might mess up my wedding speech, but I hope not to mess up our marriage.

Before returning to Jane and myself, I'm anxious to say a huge "thank you" to my mum and dad for the excellent start they've given me in life. They've said that they're proud of me today, but I'm proud of them too. They've made sacrifices to help me with my education, and as you've just heard, it's paid off. I can misquote Omar Khayyam at the drop of a hat, and throw in a line of Shakespeare for good measure.

Now, if I were to do justice to my superb choice of parents, we'd be here all night. Well, I would. You would all have gone home, and Jane would have left for the honeymoon without me. So I'll leave 99.99 recurring per cent unsaid ... You see — I know about maths as well.

Jane's parents are owed our grateful thanks too, for providing our wedding for us. We also appreciate all your thoughtfulness that has gone into it. Thank you many times over.

While on the subject of thanks, both Jane and I want you to know how delighted we are to receive all those gifts of yours. I couldn't take it in that they were all for us. This is a time when you feel grateful to have so many relations and friends. It means that all the more presents come your way. I think the only thing we haven't had is an electric toaster. It looks as though Aladdin's Cave has been emptied, and all the contents brought here.

Ken, you're prominent on the list. You've done a good job for me today. And you've done a good job for Jane. You've guided me successfully through the wedding ceremony and into Jane's arms for keeps. I could almost hear her say, "Got yer!"

I have a reservation in thanking Ken for the good job that he's done, because his speech is yet to come, and he might even mention me in it. What bothers me is that he is a chap who can get mixed up, and if he does that in his speech it might be to my detriment. Would you keep in mind that if he tells unsavoury tales about me, it's because he's getting somebody else mixed up with me.

Now, Jane and I are ambitious. We didn't simply want to get married and have a family. We wanted to get married and start a dynasty. Well, it would be nice to think that in hundreds of years time a museum guide will point to a vase and say, "This belongs to the Smith dynasty." Then probably someone will say, "Smith? That's an unusual name," and the guide will say, "It might sound unusual to you here on Mars, but it wasn't on Earth at the time."

Of course, dynasties are ruling families, and we don't particularly want to rule anybody. This touches on a subject of discussion between Jane and myself — we've spent a lot of time on serious discourse. We enjoy these exchanges together. They're like a hobby of ours. Instead of a debating society, we're a debating duo. Besides being a mutual pastime, it's helped us to understand each other. All couples discuss life, but it's invariably a half-hearted and short-lived affair, like a damp squib. However, this is not the time or place to enlarge upon the merits of the exercise of debate.

Ladies and gentlemen, I had prepared a speech, and I haven't got round to starting it yet. I'm already overrunning my time and I'm not going to impose upon you any longer. As long as I've got across to you the gratitude that Jane and I feel towards you for your participation in this happy celebration of ours, that's the main thing.

I'm not going to overlook that special "thank you" that every bridegroom must take pleasure in ending his speech with, the one directed towards the bridesmaids.

They are a most charming little group and I ask you to join with me in toasting their health and happiness.

The bridesmaids!

BRIDEGROOM No. 9

I'm very glad that I proposed to Jane, because I shouldn't have liked to miss this get-together. I'm delighted to see so many of my friends dressed up to the nines all at the same time. Well done, lads. It's in the best possible cause. I thought some of them might turn up dressed in mourning because it wasn't they who were getting married to Jane.

Well, that's got the compliment to Jane out of the way, so now I can be serious.

But seriously serious, this reminds me of my eighteenth birthday, because the spotlight was on me then, and for no other reason than that I'd survived for eighteen years. I felt then that the celebration in my honour was undeserved because reaching that age had been accomplished with little enough effort on my part. All I'd had to do was keep breathing in between eating and drinking. Yet everybody sang, "For he's a jolly good fellow!" — even if it was with an embarrassing lack of enthusiasm.

No, if anyone deserved a chorus of recognition on that day, it was my parents. They'd done all the donkey work. They'd brought me up, put me up, put up with me, fed and clothed me, supported me and pointed me in the right direction until I was able to go it alone. Even then they couldn't kick the habit.

Perhaps the tastiest fruit of their labours is for them to see me wed to this lovely girl. (TO JANE) You can say, "Here, here!" if you want to, Jane.

Many people have told me how lucky I am to be marrying Jane, including Jane. It's puzzling, because they've never explained why. Somebody will lean close to me and say in an earnest and confidential whisper, and with a bit of a nod and a wink, (ACT THIS OUT, LOOKING THIS WAY AND THAT BEFORE SPEAKING) "You're a very lucky chap to be marrying Jane!"

What does everybody know that I don't? ... My only theory to date is that it's to do with my dowry, because that's something that hasn't been mentioned yet. Perhaps I'm in for a surprise when it turns out to be a small fortune ... And there was me worrying that there might not be much left for my dowry after the provision of this wonderful feast that we've just enjoyed. It just shows how wrong you can be.

I do thank Jane's mum and dad from the bottom of my stomach for their generosity. It's been a gourmet's delight, and for me a glutton's delight. I want to thank them also for all the non-edible provisions that they have made. Mr. and Mrs. Jones have not only provided an entire wedding set-up for me, but they've thrown in their daughter as the bride.

All this means that Mum can now relax in the knowledge that her son will no longer be bringing her his socks to darn. It's been a regular thing. Every six months I've called round home with a suitcase full of socks and holes, the holes usually outnumbering the socks by about three to one. It wasn't so much the amount of darning she objected to as the smell that went with it.

But things are different now. My cases are packed for a honeymoon. One of them's full of hole-ridden socks, and darning them should find Jane something to do for the next two weeks.

It's going to be much more satisfactory for me to have a resident sock-hole mender. It really fills me with gratitude towards Mr. and Mrs. Jones for passing Jane over to me, and it's incumbent upon me to look after her with loving care for as long as she's useful.

The spotlight is on Jane today, but I want to tell you my own thoughts. It impresses upon me a strong sense of my responsibility − one that I have willingly taken on and solemnly promised to fulfil − a responsibility towards Jane. That's what today's ceremony was all about − the making of vows.

And when today is over, the spotlight will be out and the short-lived ballyhoo will have ended, but the long responsibility will have only begun, and I intend to honour it. So you see, Mr. Jones, I don't think you're going to get your dowry back.

This brings me to something else that I almost forgot. It was the idea of you wanting your gifts back that reminded me. Jane and I are so delighted with your gifts and so grateful to you for them.

Ken, to you I owe thanks for your best best-manning. I knew the job would be in capable hands.

Jane and I have been delighted by the sight of our sparkling set of bridesmaids. We'd love to have them with us every day. It's more than a pleasure for me, as my final word, to propose a toast to them.

Would you kindly join me, then, in wishing health and happiness to the bridesmaids.

BRIDEGROOM No. 10
(A globetrotter returned)

There's something special that I feel today that's making the occasion even more joyful. It's a strong sense of nostalgia, because you, my family and my old friends, with whom I've spent little enough time in recent years, have been drawn together as one party.

Being surrounded by you all after my long absences is like a breath of fresh air. It reminds me what contentment can be found without the need to wander all over the globe.

I don't regret what I did — going on distant travels — because it was an itch that had to be scratched. Better to get it out of my system as a single man than to be restless while married.

Today has brought home to me more than ever the joy of being on home ground among my own people, and as if that weren't enough, to crown it I have Jane.

"Rehabilitation" sounds a strong word, but for want of a more moderate one it describes a process that Jane is going to help me with. You see, after my nomadic lifestyle, I'm going to need some rehabilitation into the settled suburban life. I've picked up quite a few wrinkles on my travels, but they're not necessarily appropriate to the society of which I am to be a part.

Somebody could stand on a street corner shouting, "Cabbages — only £90 each!" and I'd come home and say, "Look, Jane! A street vendor was asking £90 for a cabbage but I knocked him down to £55!"

Another thing is that, varied as my worldly experience has been, I've ended up a jack-of-all-trades and master of none, just as I've acquired a smattering of several foreign languages, without fluency in any.

But it's great to be back! With Jane as my mentor, the fresh wind that I feel blowing through my life now is as sweet as any that I've felt blowing across the deck of a ship on the high seas.

Jane is the pivot of my new life and even though she looks even less like an anchor than a pivot, I see her as an anchor as well.

The days behind me were footloose and fancy-free, but now I'm walking on air. A pleasure shared is a pleasure doubled, and the pleasure for me of a settled life in the bosom of my kinsfolk is going to be not merely doubled, but multiplied a hundredfold by being shared with Jane ... well, so she says.

As you will have gathered, there is some catching up to be done on my part in domestic matters. I have to learn how to dig a garden and how to decorate a house, but I am sure that after a year or two of watching how Jane does these things, I'll get the idea.

(TURN TO JANE) And what's the other thing you keep on to me about, Jane? ... It begins with "M" ... Oh, I remember – "mortgage". That's something else of which I'm ignorant.

Talking of domestic matters I spent so much time working my passages on board ship that I've picked up some bad habits. Now when I finish a meal I must remember to wash my plate instead of looking for a porthole to push it through.

Now, I'm supposed to thank Ken publicly for his services to me as my best man and I do thank him genuinely for his capable handling of today's affairs. A best man serves not only the bridegroom, but all who attend the wedding, and you will surely agree that Ken has acquitted himself with distinction (IF BEST MAN HAS MADE A NOTICEABLE BLUNDER, QUALIFY THE LATTER STATEMENT WITH PLAYFUL EXAGGERATION, E.G. "... apart from nearly ruining the entire ceremony by ...").

To Jane's mum and dad, Jane and I give our heartfelt thanks for all that they have provided, including this wonderful reception.

My own mum and dad haven't been mentioned individually yet, but they are at the forefront of my mind. I don't know how other chaps in this position manage to convey their feelings. Every time I've arrived home after a long absence, my first meal has always been fatted calf – and every time I've said to myself, "Oh, not fatted calf again!" But it was the thought that counted and I'll simply thank mum and dad from the bottom of my heart for all their devotion to me, and hope that they believe my gratitude to them will be lifelong.

I thank you, everyone, from Jane and myself, for all those exciting gifts that have added even more to our joy today.

I'll finish now with the icing on the cake. By that I mean the bridesmaids. Well, they do look good enough to eat. Jane and I wouldn't have missed having their smiling faces with us for anything.

It's a happy note on which to end my speech by proposing a toast to those entrancing young misses.

Ladies and gentlemen, would you please raise your glasses and wish health and happiness to the bridesmaids.

BRIDEGROOM No. 11

(Bride and groom both divorcees)

It might seem a slightly unusual thing for a bridegroom to say at the beginning of his speech that he's thoroughly enjoying the occasion.

Well, I'm thoroughly enjoying this occasion and I'm happy to say so, but why might it sound at all unusual?

I think that for one thing the speech is prepared, not spontaneous and that wouldn't be something written in advance. And the thing is that until the bridegroom's made his speech he's got the thought of it on his mind and he can't properly relax, especially if he's a young man and not accustomed to speechmaking.

I know what I'm talking about because I've been in that position myself, having been married before.

It's different this time, now that I'm older and less inhibited in expressing my thoughts, and my state of mind comes from a deep assurance that the natural harmony between Jane and myself makes our match as good as any. We are both able to sit back and relax and enjoy our day to the full, knowing that, barring misfortune from the outside, we have a happy life before us.

We rejoice because we are both starting a new life. This day is not the consequence of an attitude of, "Well, we've been friends for a fair while and we seem to get along all right, so we might as well get married." If I had put that in words to Jane, it wouldn't have sounded a very enthusiastic proposal of marriage, would it? Especially if I'd dropped it out during a lull in the conversation as we were walking through a back alley and I was taking a casual kick at a dustbin in passing.

You don't have to be starry-eyed twenty year-olds to be excited at the prospect of the life ahead of you. There's such a thing as being young at heart, and the great thing about being young at heart is that you can be like it at any age. It's an attitude to life that you can adopt and cultivate no matter how old you are.

It's a trick of the trade of speechmaking to have a saying up your sleeve to underpin your message. Mine is "Today is the first day of the rest of your life."

You can vary "day" to "hour" and "hour" to "moment", and the truth remains inescapable. The present is always a new beginning, and there's nothing to prevent you from embarking on that new beginning with all the zestful anticipation normally attributed to youth.

This is the spirit in which Jane and I have gone into marriage, and in making plans for our future we have rediscovered the adventure of youth.

I have seen a dull, apathetic outlook in some couples in the springtime of their lives. I can just imagine the aforementioned dustbin serving its turn to provide a moment's stimulus in the life of the young man while he proposed.

Such people are young in their years, but not in their hearts. Jane and I are not young in our years. (Well, I'm not. I don't know Jane's age — she's never told me. In any case, arriving at a woman's age is like converting centigrade to fahrenheit. You take the age she tells you, multiply by nine over five, then add thirty-two.) But we are young in our hearts.

Well now, to come to my friend Ken here, I'd like to thank him profoundly for his services as my best man. What you have seen today of Ken's activities on my behalf — and on Jane's, really — is only part of the story. When you've had a wedding before, like Jane and myself, it's surprising the number of things involved in it that you forget about. Ken has been our salvation by bringing numerous little things to our attention.

I thank you heartily, Ken, from both of us.

Jane and I greatly appreciate everything that has been done for our benefit, and indeed all the kind well-wishing that has come our way from all quarters. It's all been very heartening to us both. It's a grand feeling to know how many sincere friends that one has.

If we'd known that we were going to receive such thoughtful and delightful gifts, we would have got married before now. We are really touched by your generosity, and we thank you very much indeed.

I can't help thinking that with such welcome gifts there's been quite a bit of advice-seeking behind the scenes as to what would please us most, and we have our children to thank for their suggestions.

That reminds me. I shouldn't like to end without a special word of thanks to them for the kind interest that they have shown in the blossoming relationship between Jane and me. Their goodwill has meant a great deal to us. We have rejoiced in knowing that they still feel close family.

Thank you, everyone, for being here. Now please carry on enjoying yourselves.

BRIDEGROOM No. 12

(From a very large family)

There may be some of you not in the family who've been thinking what a very large number of guests have been invited to this wedding. The answer is that there was a certain large group that we had to invite. That group is my brothers and sisters.

Now, you know the difficulty it is when you draw up your list of people that you'd like to have as guests, then you count them up and find out that you'll need to book the Albert Hall to accommodate them.

Your list has to be decimated in an arbitrary manner, like tossing a coin. But how can you do that with your brothers and sisters? You have to invite them all, and it doesn't stop at that. The married ones naturally have their partners with them, and their children can't be left out.

As much as we regretted it, we had to cross off the baker and the milkman and the postman. Mum and Dad are already getting stale bread, sour milk and only bills in the post.

I'm not going to hold up the proceedings by doing it, but this would have been a golden opportunity to count my brothers and sisters. This is one time that they're all in the same room and keeping still. It was never any use asking Mum and Dad how many there were of us because it only sparked off a debate between them that was inconclusive. Besides, I gave up that approach because it didn't seem fair to question Dad when he'd got his hands full already trying to cope with the reality, never mind the statistics, and I never liked to bother Mum in her condition.

Some of the neighbours' kids took advantage of our situation and gatecrashed at meal times. Mum and Dad were too busy doling out the food to notice the strangers. After this came to light, we were issued with tickets ... We had a family anthem, if you can call it that — "Happy birthday to you!" We got sick of singing it. It was nearly always somebody's birthday.

You can admire our parents for bringing so many of us into the world and rearing us. I have to admit that it's not a thing that I aspire to ... Did you hear that, Jane?

Some people go out into the world and earn medals. Others stop at home and earn them. The difference is that those who stop at home and earn them are rarely awarded them.

When a new doctor came to our house once he said to Dad, "Are these all *your* children! You should have a knighthood!" Mum said, "He's got one, but he won't wear it."

Somebody can perform a heroic act taking less than a minute and be decorated for it — quite justifiably. But there are thousands more unsung heroes and heroines whose courage and selflessness are not manifested in a sudden, meteoric burst, but are spread thinly over years. Our mum and dad are among those, and the medals they wear are invisible ones awarded to them by those who have benefited from their long heroism.

Yes, I used the word "courage", because to bring upon yourself one unknown quantity after another does take courage, and bringing upon yourself all the work and interminable tribulations of being parents of a host of offspring is selfless.

That host here assembled will all agree, and I know that they completely endorse this tribute to our mum and dad.

And now for the rest of the news. There's another set of parents that I wish to pay tribute to, and they are Jane's. What their family lacked in number compared with ours, they didn't lack in quality ... That's you, Jane.

We both wish to express our thanks to them for providing this wonderful reception for the Smith's family reunion. We are all grateful to you.

Jane and I have been overwhelmed by the seemingly endless procession of gifts that have been made to us, and for the moment all we can say is a simple but sincere "thank you". It's like suddenly having a lot of new, exciting toys to play with.

There's a gentleman here by the name of Ken who will not have escaped your notice. In case one of my brothers is called Ken, the one I mean is the one along there. To him I personally owe thanks, because he's made our special day go smoothly. Your efforts are not going unrewarded, Ken. There's a bottle of pop put aside for you to take home.

The scenes today have been enriched by our dazzling bridesmaids. They've shone like little beacons. Jane and I thank them greatly for the part that they have played so beautifully. It's a great pleasure for me to end by proposing a toast to their future health and happiness.

Ladies and gentlemen, the bridesmaids.

BRIDEGROOM No. 13

(Irresponsible ventures curbed by parents)
(Relates to Best Man's speech no. 15, on page 155.)

I'd like to say a few words first of all about Mum and Dad.

I may be stating the obvious when I say that being the parents of an adolescent is sometimes like having to deal with a monster that you've created.

I became a kind of monster, but my parents were not responsible for the blossoming of my megalomania. They worked to curb it.

It's not only the run-of-the-mill juvenile delinquents that are a bane to their parents. If they're hardened enough, they're likely to have left the suffocating nest for the fresh air of delinquent freedom. It's those that stay put that can be a burden, and not necessarily through delinquency. I was never a delinquent, but I was certainly a cross to be borne.

The difficulty for parents is in imposing their mature judgment (in my case any sane person's judgment) and steadying influence onto the madcap rising adult. My kind of blind obstinacy was in the sphere of ambition. Whereas other parents might be faced with the inertia of a layabout dropout, my parents suffered the opposite of that. My enthusiasm would run away with me, first in one direction, then another.

Not a bad thing, you may say, in a young person, but you try stemming a tide of enthusiasm that's swamping common sense and judgment.

To be fired by a novel idea can blind you to its sterility as a business venture. I was fired all right — from one steady job after another, through disrupting it and neglecting it in the consuming passion of a new dream, like starting a rumour of an imminent power strike and going round selling candles.

I chafed at the bit to initiate fresh enterprises that would reap a fortune. This is generally called ambition — a word with a narrow popular meaning if ever there was one.

Ambition covers a wider field than business. In fact it's difficult to think of anything that can't fall within it. Anything, great or small, can become the object of an individual's ambition.

I've seen on television a woman fulfilling her ambition to wash an elephant. The trouble with me was that if the idea of elephant washing entered my head, it would trigger off a grotesque process of imagination. I'd see in it the germ of a vast industry. I would reason that if elephants were washed, it was because they got dirty. Nobody wants a dirty elephant.

Here was a service waiting to be offered. Because I always thought big, my mind would leap over the common image of washing elephants in the traditional time-consuming way. I would harness modern technology. If cars could be washed by mechanical means, so could elephants. If a car wash, why not an elephant wash?

Furthermore I would set my sights on not one, but a whole chain of elephant washes throughout the country. I would open up an export market to India.

Of course, even I would know that a start had to be made in a small way. I would acquire a long mop, a bucket and a pair of step-ladders, then put an advertisement in local shop windows, including, if possible, the local pet shop. Any kind of argument that there wouldn't be sufficient demand for the service would fall on deaf ears. It would be dismissed as defeatist talk. If my parents hinted that you didn't see many elephants around, I'd say, "Of course not. People are ashamed to let them out, because they're dirty."

Well, all my grandiose schemes came to nought, and Mum and Dad's persistent pressure finally got me set on the straight and narrow path of sanity. I should like to thank them for that and for all that they've done for me ever since I've known them.

Once on that straight and narrow path, whom should I meet up with but Jane! It made the path so attractive that I never wanted to leave it. All my energy spent on crack-brained ideas was wasted and brought me nothing, but Jane was handed to me on a plate — and how tasty she looked!

Before I go any further, Jane and I would like to express our grateful thanks to her mum and dad for everything that they have provided for us, including this splendid reception.

We also want to thank all of you for your lovely gifts. It's been a great feeling receiving them, knowing the kind thoughts in which they were wrapped. Thank you, everyone.

Ken, we've all enjoyed the benefit of your finesse as master of ceremonies. Your competence and attention to my needs as my best man have put me at ease so that I've been able to enjoy the day to the full. Thank you from Jane and me.

I turn finally to our sweet bridesmaids. I have already turned to them more than once when Jane wasn't looking, and what more genuine compliment could they have than that?

Thank you, bridesmaids one and all, for being so delightful.

I'm sure everyone has been charmed by them, and it gives me great pleasure to propose a toast to their health and happiness.

Ladies and gentlemen, the bridesmaids.

BRIDEGROOM No. 14

(Marrying late in life)

It's amused me when I've met men considerably my junior but seasoned in marriage and it's come as a distinct surprise to them to learn that an old stager like me had never been married. I suddenly became an object of curiosity. Their reaction was of some incredulity with (dare I say it?) in some cases a hint of envy. (TO JANE) You didn't hear that last bit, did you, Jane?

What they found difficult to take in, so I got the impression, was that I had not been married even *once*, at my stage in life. They'd made real progress. They were already on their second or third wife.

The attitude of these chaps made me feel like a wallflower at a dance. They'd changed partners before I'd even stepped onto the floor.

Why they assumed without question that I was married puzzled me, because I always thought that I went around looking carefree.

That assumption carried through into all kinds of everyday situations. People to whom I was a complete stranger, out of the blue, referred to my "wife". Once when I was entitled to a free gift, there was something for me personally and then I was asked my wife's size in tights. I didn't like to say that I hadn't a wife, because that would have changed the subject, and there was another man behind me, waiting to pay for his petrol. Not knowing one tight from another, I acted as if I was trying to call to mind my wife's size, and as I hoped, the usual thing happened — a number was thrown at me interrogatively, and I said, "Yes".

I made my escape, wondering if it was the only size they'd got left or if I looked the sort of chap whose wife would fit that size.

This kind of thing happened all the time. If I was buying something at a store and was hesitating because there was a choice, a lady serving would say, "Your wife would like this one." ... Not only was I married, but my wife's tastes were known! These endless references to my wife half convinced me of her existence. It was me, I thought, who was suffering from amnesia.

The one kind of remark that I actually liked was, "I don't know what your wife will say when you get home!" It was one of the joys of being single. On those occasions I let fly gloatingly with, "I'm not married!"

It was whenever something was required of me that I could be caught out. A lady canvasser called at the house once and said, "Good evening. Could I speak to your wife, please?" I had started to go back into the lounge to fetch her when I remembered that I didn't have a wife. If she'd said, "Is there a lady in the house that I could speak to?" it would have been more sensible.

I wonder what's going to happen now. With a new adjustment to be made, reversing the position, will confusion still reign? If I come home and open the front door, only to have some woman throw her arms round me with protestations of undying love and of how she's missed me while I've been out to get my hair cut, will I phone for the police? Probably not, if I think Jane won't get to hear about it.

Marry in haste, repent at leisure. So goes the old saying. I hope the converse isn't true — "Marry at leisure, repent in haste." No, I think we can rule that out. As long as Jane doesn't repent, I won't.

It says a lot for Jane that I'm marrying her. When you think of all the women I've passed over, Jane must have something special. I used to dread leap year. I did think of living in a bunker for twelve months.

However, thank you, Jane, for prizing this old bachelor out of his old — bachelorhood. You have changed my life for me. I shall now be able to go round name-dropping, the name being "my wife". I shall get in first with, "My wife will kill me when I get home!" By the way, Jane, what size are your tights? That's the sort of question I shall have to be prepared for. I shall need to be alert when filling in forms. Where it says, "marital status", I must remember to put "married", and answer the questions relevant to that, such as "size of wife's tights".

Ken, I want to thank you for looking after me and for controlling today's operations so expertly. You have done well, and I'm grateful.

Now, my wife and I (notice that − not "Jane and I") have been tickled pink to be the lucky recipients of a delightful assortment of gifts. We really are grateful to you all for your kindness and generosity. We'll be chatting to you about them all in good time. Furthermore, we've been touched by all your good wishes for our future, and we thank you humbly for them.

I think that's all, so please carry on and have a good chinwag. Thank you.

BRIDEGROOM No. 15

(Bride a junior school teacher)

(This speech relates to Bride's Father's speech no. 12 on page 41.)

I should like to thank Mr. Jones for his kind warnings to me about what I might expect from Jane in our married life, if her schoolmarm officiousness carries over into our daily relationship.

I've had many years' experience of schoolteaching myself — as a pupil — and hearing that from Jane's dad gave me quite a turn. I think that my fright was a conditioned response, and the conditioning took place in my childhood.

Lost as I have been in my adoration of Jane, it had never clicked with me before now that I had gone as far as proposing marriage to one of a breed that, as a young child, I looked upon as natural adversaries in an endless battle of wits. Is that battle to be recommenced?

There will be one major difference that is a comfort. My physical stature, even though not my mental, now approximates to that of my potential opponent. Jane might be thrown off balance because the ears she's used to clipping are lower down.

You will have gathered that I was not a prize pupil. A prize idiot when it came to certain lessons, perhaps.

Some particular memories of my later days at school come back to me, like the incident with the English teacher who was forever dinning into us that we're all verbose with our first attempt at a piece of writing, and that we should keep reviewing it until we've eliminated every instance of the fault. We should, in a word, prune it.

One day this teacher grabbed me by the scruff of the neck and shot the question at me, "What do you always do to improve a piece of writing?" I said, "You prune!!" I don't think he understood English, because he ticked me off for that.

A problem at one time was overcrowding. When the girls' cookery and the boys' woodwork were going on in the same cramped room it was chaotic. Somebody made a wooden doughnut.

You hear of some funny incidents with schoolchildren, don't you? A woman shared a railway carriage with a group of girls all working away in complete silence, doing some writing as hard as they could go. She was most impressed. When she got up to leave the train she noticed what they were writing, over and over again − "I must not behave like a hooligan."

But what about the violence nowadays towards teachers! Many of them are leaving the profession for safer jobs, like the married couple who've even entered a circus. She's a knife-thrower's assistant and he's a human cannonball.

I expect we could reminisce about school for hours, but the most important thing to me about school concerns Mum and Dad. School was something they worked hard to make me take seriously. I was ushered off to it (and often propelled), in spite of the fact that I was limping with (according to my diagnosis) a broken leg, or that I'd dragged myself bravely from a sick bed to get down to breakfast.

That was one of the many things that my parents did for my ultimate benefit. I thank them for everything they've done for me, right from rocking me to sleep, to making Jane so welcome at home.

Even as I speak, the penny is dropping that part of my feeling of pride in being accepted by Jane as her life partner is the fact of her career. I hadn't realised this before, but it is a kind of achievement for me to have married a young lady such as those whose training and teaching I fought shy of as a small boy.

This achievement is not by a long way my own doing. It can be traced back to the firm hands of Mum and Dad. Indifferent as I may have been (and that applies in both ways − indifferent in ability and in interest in my own attainment), they ensured that I did not evade fulfilling my potential.

If I'd been allowed to go my own sweet way, I would hardly have turned out a suitable match for Jane.

I can foresee a misunderstanding happening repeatedly as Jane's husband, because it's already happened before. I said to somebody, "I'm waiting for my fiancée, but she hasn't come home from school yet." They gave me such a funny look.

It's going to be embarrassing when I am, say, another ten years older and I happen to speak about my wife coming home from school. People will think, "Fancy a man his age having a child bride!"

Mr. and Mrs. Jones, Jane and I want to thank you very sincerely for all that you have provided today. You have made it a splendid occasion, and we are deeply grateful.

We also want to thank everyone for all our lovely gifts. We look forward to when we can admire them at our leisure.

Finally we wish to express our appreciation of the service rendered by those young people who have contributed far more to the whole party's enjoyment than I suspect they realise — our wonderful bridesmaids.

(TO BRIDESMAIDS) Yours may have been only a walk-on part, but who could not have been delighted just seeing you walk on!

I will now ask everyone to join me in a toast to your health and happiness.

Ladies and gentlemen, the bridesmaids.

PART 5
BEST MAN'S SPEECHES

BEST MAN No. 1

You've all heard about somebody getting cold feet and not turning up at a wedding. Well, you may be surprised to learn that it almost happened with this wedding, and it was only through very determined coercion that it didn't happen. John had me by the scruff of the neck. I know it's an honour to be best man, but to some of us the thought of what can go wrong is frightening. John was asking me, "Is it ... the fear ... of losing ... the ... round ... ring?" He had to keep pausing because he was banging my head on a wall — and he didn't actually say round ring. I substituted "round" for his word that I won't repeat.

That had been one source of agitation, and some people probably can't understand why the thought of mislaying the ring should inspire such dread in the person responsible for its safekeeping. There are two reasons. It's easy enough, at the appropriate point in the service, for the bridegroom to put the ring on a finger, but the best man has to put his finger on the ring, and it's such a small object and so mobile that it's notoriously elusive. The second reason is the imagined scene if the little scoundrel has somehow given one the slip at the last moment.

Well, I had worked out a contingency plan for that. If I couldn't find the ring I was going to say to the vicar, "Oh, I know where it is. I had occasion to go into the vestry and while I was there I took it out of my pocket to give it an extra shine. I was distracted by somebody calling my name, and I put it down and walked out without it. I'll just pop and get it."

Once in the vestry I would make a furtive escape from the church, speed off to another town, stay overnight, and the next day walk into a police station and claim that I was suffering from amnesia. However, that would have caused me so much inconvenience that I thought of a better idea. I persuaded various friends and acquaintances to lend me their rings (ensuring that

I accumulated a variety of sizes) and I went into church with the proper ring in one pocket and a dozen assorted fakes in the other. If the proper ring had gone to ground when I went to fish it out, there were enough others to use. I should have passed them to John one at a time till he found one that fitted Jane's finger.

So the ring business was covered and I could dismiss it from my mind. What has given me cold feet is the thought of making a speech. I'd been trying for weeks to put one together and discovered too late that all it amounted to would take up no more than a minute — and that was with stopping half way through to blow my nose. Consequently, I must apologise for not making a speech, apart from saying something about the lad here, which is part of my brief.

What can I say about John that most of you don't already know? Quite a lot, but he wouldn't thank me for it. There is one thing I can tell you. The lads and I are surprised that he ever got near making it to the altar. He used to be so afraid of marriage that he wouldn't go out during leap year. He knew so little about the opposite sex that we gave him tuition. We started outside some toilets where they have the figure of a man on one door and of a woman on the other, and we made him play "Spot the difference".

You have the evidence today that our efforts paid off. He's hit the jackpot. It used to be John that was green and now it's us. We're green with envy. We are the hare to his tortoise in the fable.

I must admit that my ordeal of being best man has been endured happily today, because seeing Jane and John united has brought it home to me what a good cause it has been in. It's not only proud parents that are here today, but proud friends. We wish the worthy couple all the happiness that they deserve.

Turning to future brides — and my word, it is a pleasure to turn to them — I have the privilege of speaking on behalf of the bridesmaids. If Jane is today's Cinderella and John is Prince Charming, I'm afraid that the bridesmaids have no chance whatever of being the Ugly Sisters. The compliments that they have received have been so thoroughly deserved, and the thanks for fulfilling their role so delightfully. May I convey to John their appreciation of all his kind words. I'm sure they're only too happy to have been of service and to have given us all such pleasure.

BEST MAN No. 2

When John asked me if I would be his best man, I said, "Why me? You know I'm clumsy enough to bungle the proceedings." He said, "Yes, but I also know that you'd be discreet about me in your speech."

I took his point. Discretion is required by a friend of John's when talking about him to other people. However, this is no time for discretion! This is a time for revelation, warts and all ... and in your case, John, it's more warts than all.

Of course I didn't point this out to John at the time. I mean, you have to be discreet, don't you?

The very fact of John's anxiety prompted me into thinking of the shadier things about him that would hopefully be a shock to Jane and her family.

So where to start? Schooldays? That was difficult because there weren't many of them. Truant days, yes. He'd be away from school for three weeks and then tell them he'd been to the dentist's. The headmaster said to him, "Where's your dentist? On Easter Island?" John said, "I have a lot of trouble with my teeth." The headmaster said, "I know. You can't get them into your schoolwork."

The headmaster did try to see the positive side of John. He wanted him to claim a place in the Guinness Book of Records for having the largest number of dental fillings.

On one occasion, after John's longest absence, the headmaster said, "You've been away from school all this time, and you have the gall to turn up at 11 o'clock in the morning. What's your excuse for arriving so late?" John said, "I'd forgotten my way here."

It was lucky for John that the headmaster tried to do his best for him. On John's final school report he wrote, "Very good on the hole." Prospective employers thought that the headmaster had missed the "w" off the begining of the word "whole". They didn't know that there was a hole in the school yard and John had to fill it in as a punishment.

After schooldays there followed a series of escapades that were known collectively as his career. It looked very odd when he had to fill in forms and where it said "occupation" he put "escapades". At least he could spell it even if he didn't know what it meant. I was the wrong person for him to ask how to describe his occupation.

I'm turning the tables on myself a little bit now. There's such a thing as the moment of truth. This isn't it. This is a golden opportunity to be wickedly untruthful, in some things at least, and you'll be left wondering what was the truth and what wasn't. May you never know the worst. You see, I have to protect my own reputation because of the adage, "You can know a man by the company he keeps", or if you like, "Birds of a feather flock together".

I'll tell you what is a moment of truth. We've witnessed it at the ceremony today. The union of Jane and John says too much about John for my snide remarks to have any effect.

It's time I brought Jane into this because this whole affair is about John and Jane, not John and me. I think my evil desire to indulge in slander arose from jealousy. Yes, Jane — jealousy of John, because he's got you. Of all the girls that he's known, you're the one that he's chosen ... Either that or out of all the girls he's known you're the only one that would have him. Sorry! There I go again! We shall now all rise and dance the tango "Jealousy".

You, Jane, are not only a delightful young lady, but a very sensible one, and whatever unkind things I've said about John I know you will take, not with a pinch of salt, but with a ton of it. I can even hear the guests scoffing at me in their thoughts, saying, "How could *Jane* marry a lad like *that*!" ... yes, (AS AN AFTERTHOUGHT, CHANGING THE MEANING TO ONE OF ASTONISHMENT) "how *could* Jane marry a lad like that!" ... I can't stop it, can I?

I'll console myself by turning my attention to the lovely bridesmaids, one and all. On their behalf, John, I thank you for your enthusiastic compliments paid to them. They really are a colourful bouquet of flowers, aren't they? I share your sentiments about them wholeheartedly.

To finish off, may I echo the thoughts expressed between all your bachelor buddies, John, that you are a very lucky man, having wooed and won such a golden girl.

Here's to both of you. May every happiness be in store for your future.

BEST MAN No. 3

So many young chaps like myself face the prospect of making a speech with trepidation. Believe me, it is understandable. It's all right for folks who're used to it. They've gained confidence.

Now, it worried me sick when I knew that I was in for the ordeal, until I started to find out the sort of thing I was supposed to say. This opened up such a vista of opportunity that my fears were dispelled. What dispelled them was a growing excitement of malicious glee, because I was assured that I could say what I liked about the groom and he had to take it all in good part.

I got carried away with my written preparations and I looked back on an ocean of evil fiction with any semblance of truth lost beyond the horizon. The annoying thought crept in that my picture of John was so black that you kind people wouldn't believe it, so the whole thing has had to be toned down to a dull grey.

But then too many of you already know that John is neither dull nor grey. I think I'll abandon the whole idea of gratifying my sadistic streak and come clean.

John is a colourful character. This might account for my spite. I'm not colourful. But I'll allow myself a few potshots at him. After all, he's the lucky man with this beautiful bride, not me ... not that he would have wanted me, but that's beside the point.

I knew John at school and he shone, whereas I only flickered. He shone as a personality rather than as an academic achiever. I know he won't mind my saying that because he never tried to conceal his limitations on the academic side. In fact it's a joke to him. It was a joke to the school staff as well.

I remember one of John's school reports that he showed me. He'd made a name for himself at football and the sports master's comment for that subject was "Can't put a foot wrong". The maths teacher had followed this up with "Can't put a foot right." He still thinks that a square foot is some kind of physical deformity.

But we all knew that when the time came for us pupils to venture into the working world, John's qualities would carry him through ... How right we were proved! There was nobody who could empty a dustbin onto a cart like John ... Of course he had to start somewhere before he got a foot on the right ladder, ... speaking of which, he made an excellent job of that too. When he cleaned people's windows they praised him for getting in the corners. As he explained to me, it was the training he'd received at school. In the Juniors the teachers were always saying to him, "Get in the corner!".

He went to the Job Centre to see if they could find him a better job. They asked him what sort. He said, "I'd like to travel in my work", so they offered him a job as a bus driver.

One thing about John, he can certainly take a joke. So can Jane, of course. She's taken John. There's a fine spirit between them and they couldn't be better suited. When they made their marriage vows today they were both putting a foot right.

John was well prepared for courtship and marriage. In our school, biology lessons were started at an early age. We boys were given diagrams of girls and we had to colour them in.

Talking of girls reminds me of some special ones that are with us. Well, "young ladies" is a more fitting term for them. They are the bridesmaids, to whom John has gallantly paid tribute. It's my privilege to acknowledge your kind words, John, on their behalf. By the looks on their faces it was obvious that your compliments went down well with them.

Right then, before I stand down − or sit down − let me round off by saying on behalf of all John's chums as well as myself that we are extremely proud and pleased to see him wed to the lovely Jane, for whom we have such admiration. Don't get me wrong there. I didn't mean we admire her for marrying John.

Jane and John, I echo the wishes of everyone who knows you when I say all happiness to you both in your future together.

BEST MAN No. 4

(Groom a "high flier")

This is the first time I've been a best man. Thinking about it set me wondering what the record is for being best man the most number of times. Personally I have no ambition to compete for that record. My satisfaction is in performing the function for my close friend here.

I've enjoyed it all so far. That's probably because I haven't bungled anything yet — at least not so that you'd notice. (You didn't notice, did you?) The vital phase, I'm relieved to say, is successfully completed. I managed to steer John into the right church at the right time and get him married to the right bride — and the "right" in front of "bride" is the most meaningful.

Jane, you know the saying, "Behind every great man there's a woman doing something or other." This is where you come in. Keep behind John doing whatever it is in the saying. So far you have managed it and everything looks good for the future. It's been lovely weather, ideal for the photographs, and luckily for me, in fact, no serious problem has arisen.

I was told of a ghastly experience that some best man dropped in for. Can you imagine what it must be like having to struggle with somebody heavy to get him into church on time because he's paralytic drunk? And then having to hold him up all through the service? ... You'd think a vicar would know better than to get into that state before conducting a wedding, wouldn't you?

John, you know you should have been fearing this speech because it's supposed to disclose those things about you that you don't want disclosed. I'm expected to divulge murky things about your past. The reason I've been flannelling along is because there isn't enough murk that I know about. You see, Jane, he's too good to be true. He's applied himself diligently to his studies at university and it's kept him out of mischief.

Since John's been back with his old friends, we've been put to shame by the gaps in our knowledge. Conversation with John has thrown light into some of the dark corners of that ignorance. But even I knew that a man of letters wasn't a postman ... and that 'arry Stottle wasn't landlord of "The Ignorant Pig".

With all that John has in his head, it hasn't made it any bigger, thank goodness. And on the subject of heads, it's true that two of them are better than one. Now, as you see before you, there are two fine heads together. Dare I suggest that in time it will be a matter of three or four heads being better than two? I wonder if your two heads can work that out between them.

Jane and John, the world, as they say, is your oyster, and if you don't like oysters, never mind, because pearls can be gleaned from them. You are already at work on the gleaning and producing pearls of wisdom.

Mentioning pearls reminds me of a small, but very decorative string of them, the sight of which has given us all great pleasure today. I refer to the bridesmaids, whom John has so rightly praised.

It falls to me to thank you, John, on their behalf, for what you said.

I think that's all, so I'll close with the wish that Jane and John have all *their* wishes come true.

BEST MAN No. 5

When John first asked me if I would be his best man my reaction was, "Why me? The best man has to make a speech, doesn't he, and I don't know you as well as some of the others do." He said, "That's why I'm asking you."

That in itself made me think that it would be more fun sitting out there with you and listening to the best man's speech instead of delivering it. But John was insistent and was so agitated that out of sympathy I gave way.

What neither of us knew at the time was that when I set about preparing my speech, knowing now that there were skeletons in John's cupboard, it was only natural for me to want to find them and so approach the very people who knew about them, his other friends.

This I did, but before you panic, John, I shall not reveal all, but instead confine myself to some of your lesser secrets.

There's one great thing that John has done that we have to give him full marks for and it's staring us in the face. He has married Jane. And you, Jane, when you've had an earful of what's coming in the next few minutes, will get full marks if you're still sitting there and haven't run off to enter a convent.

Through no fault of his own John suffered a long spell on the dole. He became a bit desperate and started to think up grandiose fund-raising schemes.

The atmosphere became distinctly sinister when he held so-called social gatherings in his flat. They always started late at night and a light could still be seen on well into the early hours of the next day. It was all hush-hush. Those who attended were forbidden to speak about it. That was understandable. People might laugh if they knew that a young man was holding Tupperware parties.

John's drive to save wherever he possibly could became a mania. Somebody gave him an old bicycle to get around on and he walked everywhere to avoid the wear on the tyres. Many a time in the winter he would sit warming himself round a lighted match. When there was nothing else to do he used to go into the park and hang about by the duck pond, waiting for people to throw bread.

Not that John was a mean person, but in the end things became so bad that he applied to withdraw some money from his Swiss bank account. There was some mix-up there and he had to throw himself on the mercy of the Social Security. He went down on his knees to them, begging and pleading. In the end they gave in and paid his air fare to Zurich to go and sort things out.

One of John's more recent enterprises has been to tour Greenland and Lapland warning people to be prepared for the greenhouse effect. He's made a fortune selling mops and buckets to eskimos. Then there'll be all his commission on the orders he got for refrigerators. When he went round with his banner, "BE PREPARED", the eskimos took him for a Boy Scout. They thought it must be "bob-a-job" week and he'd come to see if they wanted their snow swept.

John didn't look as though he would ever marry, but we lads thought it was what he needed. We thought he was too disorganised and wayward in his life and that he needed an anchor ... We told him this, so he went out and bought one. You see what I mean?

Eventually we managed to drum the message home, and one day he stood looking thoughtfully into the distance, and said, "Yes, I think you're right. I should have some sensible young woman to keep me on an even course. Somebody that I have to answer to, if you like. Somebody that I can come home to and who'll have my dinner ready. Somebody who'll wash up afterwards, and do my washing and ironing, and do the shopping ... and slave over a hot stove all day and work her fingers to the bone while I put my feet up on the mantelpiece ... Yes, my mind is made up. I'll get after that Jane Jones and see if I can crack it with her."

Today you have all gathered together to celebrate his success.

We lads are greatly fond of John, and now that he is departing from our bachelor midst we must try to comfort ourselves with the thought that we are not losing a friend, but gaining a Jane.

Looking at it like that, what a bargain we've got!

Talking of a bargain, there are some special goodies on display today with a "sell by" date far in the future, but none of them will be left on the shelf. I refer to the bridesmaids. It is my pleasure to speak on their behalf and to thank John for kind words in their direction.

Finally, the lads and I congratulate you, John, on the best thing you ever did — and on getting married.

You're in good hands now. Here's to both you and Jane for lifelong happiness.

BEST MAN No. 6
(Groom a civil servant)

To put first things first I'd like to say a few words about someone who is playing a key role in today's event — myself. I am very important and my extensive contribution to the running of the proceedings should not be underestimated.

I know that because it's in a letter to me from Auntie Annie — in reply to my request for information on a best man's duties that I sent to her Advice Column.

However, I should like to say from the start something that's nothing to do with that lady's advice. It gives me a warm feeling inside to see my friend John with Jane as his bride.

I don't know whether it was his charm and good looks that worked the oracle, or the more likely agent, that black cat in the neighbourhood that tried to live up to the reputation of bringing good luck.

Not that John is undeserving. Our parents' generation are forever complaining about the disappearance of standards and values in all walks of life, but John has begun his chosen career well by insisting upon a revival of the traditions of the Civil Service. He insists upon observing a proper morning tea break … That's one of his two main priorities. The other is the *afternoon* tea break.

He learned his lesson from when he went for his interview. At first he was considered unsuitable because he put his foot right in it. They asked him if he'd like some tea, and he said "No, thank you." He hadn't heard about the Civil Service magazine — "One lump or two?".

Mind you, he favours innovations that allow employees more latitude, such as flexi-time, where you can work over on one day if you want to leave early the next. He's calculated that if he worked through his tea breaks for the next two years he'd be able to retire when he was 39.

Another Civil Service tradition is doing everything in triplicate. Jane might be happy about the thought of twins, but beyond that could be a different matter. There's an annual concert and John's already booked (NAME OF SINGING TRIO OR "A SINGING TRIO") as the soloist.

Yes, it's not all work and no play in the Civil Service. Their social side is very active. They have darts and snooker and table tennis, a debating society, amateur theatricals ... plenty to keep themselves occupied until it's time to go home.

But that triplicate business can be a menace. What about when there's a typing error? It once meant there were three bridges built across a river where there shouldn't even have been one!

However, the Civil Service does have an air of respectability and I've noticed the influence on John. When he stands aside to let a lady pass, he goes through the doffing the hat business (GO THROUGH ACTION OF DOFFING HAT) ... I don't know why, when he's not wearing a hat ... It makes him look a silly doffer.

He has started to overdo things rather. You've seen him today in his top hat and tails (OR OTHERWISE "SMART SUIT"). That's what he wears for gardening.

The lads and I have noticed little changes in his behaviour — like scratching his nose with an umbrella ... and when we're all walking along the street, he makes us keep twenty paces behind him.

Of course there's really nothing wrong with raising one's own standards. It's unfair to call it pretentiousness. When Jane agreed to marry John, he straight away started scouring the papers for somewhere to live ... I say papers, but in fact it was a Guide to English Stately Homes.

When John goes on holiday, we shouldn't be critical just because he sends a postcard to the Royal Family ... any more than we should be derisive because he wanted to be chauffeured when he went on the bumper cars. It's a matter of standards. When he and Jane enter their home for the first time as man and wife, he'll get the butler to carry her over the threshold. The gnomes in his garden won't be plastic ... They'll be real.

We friends of his from our younger days are not surprised at the promise he's showing in his work because he always had a happy knack of using initiative.

Sometimes things rebounded on him, like the time that we accidentally burned somebody's shed down when we went round clearing people's snow away ... It was John's idea to take a flame thrower. Then there was the time that he led the way on a hiking holiday in Wales, and we got into trouble for trespassing when we took a short cut — through somebody's cottage.

Well, John, I hope Auntie Annie would be satisfied with this. She did say I was to jest at your expense.

Turning to some other very attractive young people here, apart from yourself, John, I noted your choice of words for the bridesmaids. Auntie Annie called them my charges and said I should speak for them, so please accept their thanks for what you said. They've helped to make your day, but I think you've made theirs.

Thank you.

BEST MAN No. 7

(Bride and groom very young)

The other night, when I was at John's stag party, looking at the very youthful bridegroom-to-be, I was reminded of another drinking bout that I'd been forced to take part in. One very young chap there was newly engaged. I think that was what we were supposed to be celebrating, but as far as everybody was concerned, it was the drinking that mattered, not the excuse for it.

When the hour was mellow, a chap called Peter said to the engaged one, Ian, (DRUNKEN VOICES FOR BOTH MEN) "Albert, why are you and Marie getting hitched so young?" Ian said, "Well, Archie, you know me. Any excuse for a party." Peter said, "You mean you decided to get married so that we could have this binge! ... Good idea!" Ian said, "No. Not this party. A Diamond Wedding party."

Jane and John are probably getting married early to make sure of a Diamond Wedding celebration. It must have been that bit in a newspaper that I pointed out to John of a couple getting married in their eighties. They didn't look like making it to the Diamond Wedding.

From time to time we do see a newspaper photograph of a couple enjoying that celebration. Jane and John, I must warn you that you'll look like them when your turn comes. Just imagine yourselves — the baldness, the wizened face, the scruffy beard ... and that's just Jane.

Do you know the name of the anniversary when you've been married for seventy-five years? No kidding, there is one, and do you know what it is? It's Diamond, just the same as for the sixtieth one. It's because they think if you go on for that long you'll be past any recollection that you had a Diamond Wedding fifteen years before.

Talking of photographs, this is probably the only wedding that John has attended which won't yield a crop of grotesque ones because for once he hasn't brought his camera. If I describe John as an amateur photographer I mean "amateur" rather than "photographer".

I can't help suspecting a fault in the manufacture of the lens in that camera of his. If only that accident could be reproduced, it would reap a fortune for the makers for its comic creations. All you have to do is take a snap of somebody in the ordinary way, and the print shows them with one foot three times as large as the other — and the other's already twice its normal size.

I took his first snap of me back to the shop. I said, "When we asked for them to be enlarged, we meant the whole picture, not my feet."

When the subject of my speech cropped up between us and my obligation to discuss him, John said that I could tell the truth, the whole truth and nothing but the truth — as long as I restricted myself to the good things about him. Because a one-minute speech would seem ridiculous, that's why I've had to waffle on so much.

One thing about John is that, whatever he does, he always lands on his feet. I first heard this said by the diving instructor when he went swimming at school. A dancing partner of his said something similar — "Whatever dance we do, he always lands on my feet." ... If she'd seen my feet on that photograph she'd have thanked heaven she wasn't dancing with me!

We can't get away from feet with John, can we? He's even gone into marriage feet first, and if there's one thing above all where he's landed on them, it's this. (TO JANE) Don't you agree, Jane? Just blush and giggle. You don't need to say anything. (BACK TO GUESTS) I wish I'd saved that for the end of my speech. It would have made a good footnote.

To be serious for a minute, thinking about the close devotion of Jane and John, a verse comes back to me — I forget which poet it's by — which expresses that, describing a poignant moment of parting. It would be apt to substitute Jane and John's names in it. (PRETEND TO CONCENTRATE ON RECALLING THE LINES)

Jane stood at the doorstep,
As John walked down the street.
Her heart was full of sorrow,
And her boots were full of feet.

Thank you, John, for brightening up the day for the bridesmaids with those teasing flatteries of yours. They don't make speeches, so I have to speak for them. May they be as lucky in love as Jane.

(BACK TO GUESTS) That's me about finished, and I hope I haven't put my foot in it.

I wish our couple every happiness, and hope that it won't be too long before they hear the patter of tiny feet.

BEST MAN No. 8

(Groom works in a tailor's shop)

I won't speak for too long because John's got to get our suits back to the shop. I think the only reason he started to work at that so-called tailor's was so that he could borrow his wedding outfit.

He's got to get them back because they're booked for later on today. There's a bridegroom and best man somewhere, anxiously biting their nails as they stand at a window in their underclothes watching out for some manifestation of the tailor's fast delivery service.

It is to be hoped that the chain doesn't come off that lad's bike again ... It's not so much the delay, it's the oil he gets all over his hands putting it back on. If they'd only wrap the suits up as a precaution, it would save a lot of trouble. But then what can you expect of a shop that doesn't even take care not to mix up its orders?

There is one thing to be said for them. They're not humourless. They see the funny side of their mistakes. They keep an album of wedding photographs to display their wares. One of them shows a bridegroom with trouser bottoms six inches above his ankles and a jacket so large that page boys are having to hold up the tails. Fortunately he couldn't see himself in a mirror in the complete rigout, because the hat covered his eyes.

I don't know about outfitters. They're the strangest outfit I've ever known ... They held a sale and claimed that everything in the shop was reduced. All that week the manager was only four foot tall.

During the sale an assistant's glasses were broken in the crush, but he carried on and took the waist measurement of a man who wanted some trousers. When he tried them on he said, "These are no good to me! You could get two people inside these!" The assistant had put the measuring tape right round him and another customer at the same time.

A contortionist once went in and described to John a weird and wonderful jacket that he wanted for his act. It was something that an audience wouldn't believe anyone could get into, and he wondered if they could possibly make it. John said, "That's no problem, sir ... Just help yourself off the rack."

The time it takes to get a suit made up from there is unbelievable. They claim that all their made-to-measures are bargains. I ordered one from them that was costing me £240, and I said to John, "I don't see how it's a bargain." He said, "It is. With inflation, by the time you get it, it'll be worth four hundred."

You can imagine that life isn't dull in John's company. Life is full of surprises and John is full of life, so John is full of surprises. To us pals of his the biggest surprise of all has been Jane. I don't mean Jane herself was a surprise. I mean John dating her was, because previously he had freely indulged a whim for going out with weirdos.

When we first heard about Jane, we imagined, from John's record, that she'd have spikes instead of hair, bags painted under her eyes, graffiti on her forehead, earrings looking like bicycle wheels on lavatory chains, probably wearing an overcoat under a miniskirt, luminous yellow tights, and with a black handbag that she could pop a spare pair of wellingtons in.

For all we know, Jane might have been like this when John first met her. That would explain his initial attraction to her. If that's so, it's a good job she changed, because he couldn't have kept her in chewing gum.

John's never known this, but we held a competition between ourselves to see whose vision of a girl came nearest to the one that he ultimately married. We each wrote out descriptions of what we envisaged and one of us sketched pictures from the descriptions. If you're interested in seeing them, we can show them to anybody who's over sixteen ... No, I'm only kidding, John. Anybody can see them.

Now, what attracted Jane to John? Could it have been his exploits in the field of salesmanship? After all, that shop is a hotbed of it. At any other tailor's if you buy a suit from them, they persuade you to buy a tie to go with it. At John's place, if you buy a tie, you come out with a suit to match it.

Well, that's all the true stuff. I had intended to do some leg-pulling as well, but I think I've spoken for long enough, so if you'll excuse me I'll finish off.

What better way to do so than on the subject of those young treasures, the bridesmaids? It's my privilege to acknowledge John's thanks to them for their service, and I do that with pleasure.

Jane and John, my last word is to wish you your full share of life's happiness.

BEST MAN No. 9
(Rural area, groom originally a "townie")

When I first knew John, it was when his family came to live here from the town, and as we became friendly I honestly thought, (BROAD LOCAL ACCENT) "We've got a right one 'ere!"

Being country born and bred myself I couldn't take it in that anybody could be so ignorant of the country.

On his first visit to our farm, John said, "Ken, do you feed your cows enough? Look, they're eating the grass." When he saw a flock of sheep he said, "Why are those animals all following each other like sheep?" He thought a cowpat was something you did to show your approval if they'd given a lot of milk.

He couldn't get used to being wary of this danger and he kept stepping into it. He didn't think the bells of the village church went "Ding-dong!" but "Ding-dung!" — because that was how he'd always heard it pronounced in Birmingham. He imagined there was a lookout on the church tower and the bells rang to warn people every time a cow deposited some danger.

When we said that the yew tree was going to come down, he thought somebody was going to demolish a pub.

What puzzled him in his early days was why we other kids in his class were talking to each other in attempts at his dialect, and laughing.

Gradually his manner of speech changed under our influence, and now it's a bit of a hybrid.

Fortunately he stopped asking questions like, "Are there any yokels about?" and "Where does the village idiot live?"

When he asked that question of people he was given quite a variety of addresses.

John enlightened me about some of the differences he found. One of them was that where he lived before, the postman used to push seaside cards through the letter box without stopping to read them.

He observed how people here found time to chat to each other during the course of their daily round. In the town potatoes were something you ate. Here they were a topic of conversation. Eggs were things you bought at a grocer's shop. Here they seemed to be everywhere. Even the hens ate so many of them that they came out of their behinds.

Something else that challenged his credulity when he first arrived was the bus service. In the town, when they talked about the bus service, they meant the *service*. Here we meant the *bus*. It niggled him why he never saw two buses passing in opposite directions. It was a long time before he twigged that there was only one bus.

One day he ran for it and just missed it. He asked somebody what time the next one was due and they said, "On Thursday."

I suppose our pace of life must have seemed strange to a young boy straight from the hustle and bustle of town. There was a certain old gentleman that John saw setting off on foot up the lane. One of the villagers said, "That's old Mr. So-and-so going to the hairdresser's." John said, "But his hair's short." They said, "It won't be by the time he gets there." ... When his funeral cortege passed, it was the fastest he'd ever been.

John's image of the countryside was limited by all the pastoral pictures that he'd seen. He expected to see all the girls past school age dressed as dairymaids and in the company of cows. He didn't believe that one of them worked in a bank.

Well, John himself is a commuter. To that degree he hasn't been absorbed into what he would call the mud and muck.

Jane, you know what you've done, don't you? You've married one of those townie foreigners.

Incidentally, I think I've spoken long enough and I haven't got round to the fascinating revelations I was going to make about you, Jane. I apologise to everyone for that. It can wait till your Silver Wedding party. You know what we're like round here. Time's no object.

There was a time when John would most likely have imagined bridesmaids at a country wedding tramping manure into the village church. I think that at least he's passed that stage. By what he said about Jane's bridesmaids he implied that they'd taken a fragrance in — and they had.

I'm sure that they would like to make a vocal acknowledgement themselves, but tradition demands that they use a spokesman. That's me. So, John, consider yourself thanked by them.

Jane and John, I wish you every happiness, and John, when you go out of here, just mind where you tread while you're in your wedding shoes.

BEST MAN No. 10

(Groom of Scottish descent, nervous type)
(Relates to Bride's Father's speech no. 9 on page 32.)

I don't suppose there's anyone here more relieved than I am that this hour has arrived. You wouldn't believe how on edge John has been. Even if we were alone, he'd speak in urgent whispers as if he were scared of being overheard.

It's worried me because if we'd been observed, it would seem as though we were planning a robbery instead of preparing for a wedding. John's even referred to the rehearsals in church as a dummy run.

Can you imagine what it's like when you meet in the street and before he starts talking to you he takes a furtive look round and then speaks out of the side of his mouth?

As soon as he snaps, "I've got it!" he's got me looking round anxiously and glancing up to check if there are any police spy cameras pointing at us.

Next thing, he fishes something out of his pocket. I can't see what it is because his fist is tightly clenched round it. Then with a sudden movement it's passed to me, and John's looking tense and grim. By pure reflex action I take the mysterious something and slip it into my pocket before anybody notices.

If a policeman had suddenly appeared and asked us the time, I should have bolted. As it was, I'd only taken possession of a small box containing the wedding ring.

Then in the evening came the telephone call, and the anxious question barked at me, "Is it in a safe place?" I said, "Yes, it's in Paris." He said, "What are you talking about?" I said, "The Eiffel Tower. What are you talking about?"

No, actually I tried some reassurance. I said, "I'm not going to tell you where the you-know-what is over the phone in case anybody overhears." That impressed him. Its location was, in fact, where it would never enter the heads of either the police or a rival gang that it would be. It was hanging on a hook in the kitchen cupboard.

The ring should really have resided in John's keeping until this morning, but he wanted me to safeguard it.

If he himself had been abducted before the wedding, I don't think he'd have worried as long as the ring was safe. In fact, if Jane had been abducted I don't think he'd have worried as long as the ring was safe.

It's become such a fixation with him that it could carry on even now that the ring is on Jane's finger. If she does get kidnapped on the honeymoon I can see John in panic offering a reward for the safe return of the ring. He might reason that as long as he had the ring back, he could always look for another bride to fit it. He could get a new bride for nothing, but he'd have to pay for a new ring.

It's the Scottish blood in him. He had to be persuaded to take Jane somewhere abroad for the honeymoon. He wanted to spend it in this hotel to save travelling expenses. When he finally did enquire at the travel agency about a honeymoon hotel, he asked for a reduction because there'd be two of them sharing a room.

The reason he was smiling so broadly when the photographs were taken outside the church was because it was the first wedding he'd been to where he could walk out without putting any money on the plate.

He's so proud of being Scottish that he's packed something patriotic to hang on the wall of their room when he gets to the hotel. It's a notice that says "NO TIPPING ALLOWED".

Jane, your dad has highlighted your virtues as a secretary, so with your cool command over people and situations, things can be left in your capable hands from now on — at least as soon as I've got you both safely into the car for your exit from the scene. What happens to you both on your journey isn't my responsibility — and something will happen, because the car's been "fixed". It was part of my duty to organise a joke on the bride and groom for their departure, and I haven't failed in my duty.

Of course, I'm not going to be a spoilsport and say what's been done. You can phone the A.A. if you like, but don't phone me. I just want to relax and enjoy myself and forget all about being a best man.

If there's one thing I'm not joking about, it's my pleasure in speaking for the bridesmaids and thanking you, John, for the good wishes that you have expressed for them.

Jane and John, have a wonderful married life.

BEST MAN No. 11
(Groom with acting experience)

Keeping company with somebody who's dabbled in amateur dramatics, like John, can be disconcerting. An act can be put on in order to deceive.

Before this makes Jane put her thinking cap on, let me put her mind at ease. Acting usually involves the spoken word, and this is John's weakness. Not that he can't speak convincingly on stage. He can — if he remembers what to say. The memory trouble blights his off-stage acting just the same.

Jane, if John wanted to fool you by saying, "I've had enough of you! Get out of this house!" he'd go (DO APPROPRIATE ACTION, LOOKING FIERCE, POINTING AT DOOR, THEN PUTTING HAND TO HEAD TRYING TO THINK OF THE WORDS. THEN) "I ... I ... I've ... I've ... I've had ... ".

If he does remember his lines straight off, he's so surprised that he gets confused with his stage directions, so he'd probably go, "I've had enough of you! Get out of this house!" (POINT ALL THE WAY ROUND, TRYING TO REMEMBER WHERE THE DOOR IS)

I'll say this for him. He's a trier. When he first started, he dedicated himself to hard work as the path to success. Wherever he went, he could he heard constantly rehearsing, "To be ... or not to be ..." It was a pity he could never remember any more of that speech.

People overhearing him could be so cruel! They used to call, "Next!"

Even when we go into a pub he forgets his lines. The gang of us can be at the counter and we have to prompt him — (STAGE WHISPER) "Four pints, please."

We had to take precautions for today's ceremony. What you didn't see, but what I can tell you now is that the vicar had an idiot board shoved up his cassock with "I DO" chalked on one side and "I WILL" on the other.

(NOW, WITH REFERENCE TO THIS THEME, SOMETHING MAY BE SAID ABOUT THE SPEECH THAT JOHN HAS MADE. IF HE HAS BUNGLED IN ANY WAY, JOKE ABOUT IT. IF NOT, THEN SAY,

"He must have made his speech up as he went along, because if it had been prepared he wouldn't have remembered it.")

But all the world's a stage, and we've seen some interesting action on it in our own little corner of the world today. John must have finally come out with, "Will you marry me?" after rehearsing it, at least in his mind, as many a young man does if he's the shy type. Knowing John, though, if he did get those four words out in one go, he probably put emphasis where it shouldn't have been, and Jane would be faced with the question, "Will *you* marry me?" with the implied clause, "because nobody else will." Then again it could have been, "Will you marry *me*?" as though she was thinking about marrying somebody, and John wanted to know if it was him, so that he could announce his engagement.

Anyway, the deed is done. Now, Jane and John, you can look forward to wedded bliss. Absolutely nothing but pure, unadulterated bliss from morning till night for the rest of your married life ... You can look forward to it, but you won't get it.

Getting married under the delusion that you're setting yourself up for a wonderfully happy, carefree time is like booking a holiday expecting the paradise promised in the travel brochure. It isn't all basking in the sun on soft, golden sands. It's sometimes having to mop up after the rain that's poured through the hole in the hotel roof.

I'm speaking from experience — the experience of millions of happily married people.

I should warn John that in order to achieve a state of affairs as blissful as possible he should mend his bachelor ways. Accustomed as he is to having only himself to answer to in his flat, he will now have to adjust to a new régime.

Someone will notice if he leaves his socks lying about the bedroom floor. It'll be no use him saying, "They're not mine", as he might have done when he lived with other male sock wearers in the family home.

Of course, that cuts both ways. I don't know whether Jane's

untidy, but if John picks up a pair of knickers that are lying about, it's going to pose a difficult question if Jane says, "They're not mine."

Other little things John will have to watch are that he transfers his porridge into a dish instead of eating straight out of the saucepan — and washing up after meals instead of putting all the things in together at the end of the week, when he has a bath.

Before finishing, I should like to unburden myself of a feeling of guilt about some exaggeration on my part. In fairness I should tell you that the vicar didn't really have an idiot board under his cassock. It was only a piece of paper.

I'm glad John didn't have to remember that line. He might have said that the vicar had an idiot under his cassock.

Finally, John, on behalf of the bridesmaids, I thank you for your good wishes to them wrapped up in that pretty little speech. Those young ladies can take my word for it that that was no make-believe. As the saying goes, I couldn't agree more with your sentiments.

BEST MAN No. 12

(Bride and groom divorcees. In Scotland, bride's homeland. Groom a commercial traveller.)

Before I set about saying what I have in mind, I must tell you that I feel wary about it because I'm not on home territory.

Don't take that wrongly. You see what I mean. I've probably put my foot in it from the start. Why I feel a bit awkward is because here I am, along with John and the rest of his retinue, whom I can insult with impunity, also in the company of a large number of Jane's people. If I say anything sarcastic, albeit in fun, about this part of the globe, I might get a haggis thrown at me before I have a chance to close my mouth.

If that did happen, I'd stuff some of it in my pocket and have it analysed when I got back to England. I know there are two "g's" in "haggis", but I don't know what else.

The trouble is that we English love to make jokes about the Scots. That's all right south of the border, because we have safety in numbers. If my tongue slips I entreat you good, kind Scots people to forgive me. If you don't, I shall make you scatter. I'll say, "Ooh, look! Here's a charity collector!"

John's very naive about Scots people. At least he used to be. I can remember being with him on a railway station in our younger days and a train came in from Edinburgh. He couldn't understand why the driver and fireman weren't wearing kilts. I had to get him to imagine what would happen in the rush of wind when they got speed up.

Talking of trains, John's commercial travelling did once bring him to Scotland. He had an appointment in London and he boarded a train in Birmingham that was going the wrong way.

Of course, I knew John when he first started as a commercial traveller — going from door to door selling brushes. He couldn't afford a vehicle, so he had to carry an entire day's stock with him to each house. It was a good job they were toothbrushes. His only customer was an old woman with no teeth who bought one to get rid of him.

His next house-to-house venture was with hearing aids. He got his foot in one door and managed to gabble on with his sales talk for ten minutes to the old man who was there ... It didn't do any good. The poor chap was deaf.

What he should have stuck to was the new brand of electric light bulbs. He sold some to a wayside hotel and booked a room for the night. During the evening he and some other guests played snooker in an old lumber room that was never used. It came back to him when he was passing the hotel ten years later, so he called in for a drink and asked the manager if he remembered anything about it. The manager said, "Oh, yes! I remember! I went in that room this morning. You'd left the light on."

Now, I have some advice for Jane and John for their married life ... I know what they're thinking — "Who's he to give us advice when we've both been married before?" Well, there are things in their new situation that they won't have experienced already. You see, Jane and John, when you were married before, you hadn't been married before.

Through habit from their previous marriages there will be instances of each of them getting their present partner mixed up with their former one.

To make my point, have you ever thought what must happen with Hollywood stars who've married several times?

Fancy the wife turning over in bed in the morning and saying, half asleep, (AMERICAN ACCENT) "Time you got up and fixed me some corfee, you lazy, good-for-nothing Charles, Henry, Eddie, Bob, Hal, Rick, or whatever your name is!"

Just when they've got used to the one partner's likes and dislikes, they have to get used to another's. The arguments it could cause! — "You always said you liked stewed oranges dipped in gravy, you ungrateful wretch! Why don't you make your mind up!"

So my advice to our happy couple is to keep reminding themselves who they are, otherwise they might think they're a different couple altogether.

Another thing to be prepared for is the minor hazards in

communication that will occur from time to time because of unexpected differences in dialect and pronunciation. English people fail to use the proper Scots pronunciation even of something simple like "loch". Instead they say "lock". As a child, John was afraid to go along by a canal in case he met the Lock Ness Monster.

Here's an example of how we've lagged behind you in education. Some of us see a characteristic of some of your countrymen as being what we describe as dour. We say, "He's a dour Scot." But a little lad in school told to use the word twice in one sentence to bring out in full the fine subtleties of its meaning said, "Ower 'ouse 'as got a front dour and a back dour."

It's been grand to come up here onto Scottish soil, and I wish Jane and John every happiness, whatever soil they're on.

BEST MAN No. 13

(Bride and groom divorcees, groom Welsh.)

There's one thing that has made it no difficult task for me to say my piece on this occasion, and that is that I've known John for a very long time.

I can vaguely remember the first time that John and I met. He was bending over a pram doing a lot of incomprehensible baby talk. Well, it was incomprehensible to me, and I was the baby. It would have been difficult enough to understand in any case, but as it was delivered in what I learned later was a Welsh accent, the difficulty was compounded.

The speech you hear from John now is something that has benefited from the civilizing influence of moving amongst English people.

It wasn't the accent alone, but in John's more primitive days he'd greet you with, (WELSH ACCENT) "Good morning, isn't it?" — and I suppose it was if you liked being out when it was bucketing down.

I've been to John's corner of the land of his fathers, and it's no wonder I found him hard to understand. The people in his village did as well.

I gathered that he had an unfortunate way of using his own vernacular. A very broadbottomed Mr. Jones was the village grocer. To distinguish him from the thirteen other Joneses, John referred to him as "Jones the backside".

He passed a woman in thick fog one night and couldn't recognise her, so he called, "Good night, Mrs. Jones or Mrs. Evans or Mrs. Thomas, indeed to goodness!" When she got home her husband said, "Did you meet anybody else out?" She said, "Only (BRIDEGROOM'S SURNAME) the pratt."

I used to have trouble pronouncing Welsh place names. As a lad I spent three weeks at Llanfairfechan. When people asked me where I'd been camping I said, "Cardiff."

But isn't the Welsh singing voice beautiful? I'll never forget one moonlit night, walking back to camp and hearing a male voice choir that had just filtered out of the village pub. They'd chosen the old song, "Boiled beef and carrots".

Now, John might be getting a bit long in the tooth, but he must still have his wisdom teeth. He was wise enough to know what he was doing, proposing to Jane, having experienced a failed marriage. Mind you, he won't have things all his own way, because Jane's had experience of the vicissitudes of marriage.

John will have learned by his mistakes. This time he won't sing in his bath. Can you imagine what it was like for his first wife? She could never have a clean husband without having to endure, "We'll keep a welcome in the hillsides." And he wouldn't be satisfied with a little rubber duck in the bath. It had to be a red dragon.

For another thing Jane will be able to watch a programme on old English fairy cakes while there's a rugby match being televised from Cardiff Arms Park.

Perhaps I should be more circumspect in the presence of John's compatriots, in case anything is taken amiss. People are inclined to make fun of what they're ignorant about, and there's so much about Wales where I've been ignorant. At school I thought that Merthyr Tydfil was a dinner lady.

Jane, think what a delight it's going to be when John takes you to his homeland and shows you around some of the breathtaking scenery that can be enjoyed by Welshmen day in and day out ... Have you ever been down a coalmine?

(THE DIALOGUE IN THE FOLLOWING TWO PARAGRAPHS SHOULD BE DELIVERED IN AN EXAGGERATEDLY WELSH MANNER. IT SHOULD BE QUITE UNHURRIED, DELIBERATE AND EMPHATIC)

That reminds me about a man in the Rhondda Valley who came home from work and his wife said, "Ooh, look at you, Evan! − all covered in coal dust from head to foot!" The next day when he got home his wife said, "Ooh, look at you, Evan! − all covered in coal dust from head to foot!" The following day, in he walked from work, and what did he hear but, "Ooh, look at you, Evan! − all covered in coal dust from head to foot!" Evan said, "Listen, Gladwyn, look you! When I came home

from work on Monday you said, 'Ooh, look at you, Evan! —
all covered in coal dust from head to foot!' When I came home
from work on Tuesday you said, 'Ooh, look at you, Evan! —
all covered in coal dust from head to foot!' Now I've just come
home from work again and you've said, 'Ooh, look at you, Evan!
— all covered in coal dust from head to foot!' Why do you say
it, Gladwyn?" She said, "Well, you *are* a *milkman*!"

And if that isn't Irish, I'm a Dutchman!

The best of British luck to you both!

BEST MAN No. 14
(Bride a nurse, groom a doctor)
(Relates to Bride's Father's speech no. 11, on page 38.)

First of all I should like to tell you about a camping holiday I was on with some other lads. We'd gone for a walk and entered a wood. We were deep into it when one of the group tripped and fell, hurting himself badly. We did what we could but he was in considerable pain, and one worried chap said, "Perhaps we should look for a nurse." We said, "Don't be silly! Whoever thought of looking for a nurse in a wood!" ... But we found a nurse ... and we found a doctor, too.

And that is how I first met Jane and John ... because we were later introduced to them by that doctor and nurse.

I've found it interesting listening to John talk about his work. Diagnosis often presents difficulties, and demands astute detective work in medical science to arrive at a conclusion.

John was once faced with a most dirty, unkempt, slovenly young woman, and during his examination of her he stopped and said very thoughtfully, "How long have you been married?" She said, "Why?" He said, "There's some confetti in your ear."

As a raw recruit to his profession John was naive in some of his diagnoses and suggested treatments.

A fellow student acted as a patient and they started John off with the most trivial complaint they could think of. The "patient" complained of a tingling sensation in his right leg. John said, "It's pins and needles. Amputate the leg immediately." They said, "Why?" He said, "To save it spreading to his left leg."

I remember when I went to the doctor's with an extremely sore throat, and my voice was really hoarse. It had come on badly late in the day, and I was anxious to catch the doctor before surgery closed, so I hurried round. When I arrived the place was deserted, so I knocked on a door, and it was opened by a young receptionist. I said, (STAGE HOARSE WHISPER, SLOWLY) "Is the doctor in?". She said, (STAGE WHISPER, FURTIVELY) "No. Come on in."

I love it when a doctor has an appropriate name, don't you? − like the surgeon, Bertram Frederick Brown. Patients were worried when they saw his name written − "B.F. BROWN". A meaningless coincidence like that can, by mere association of ideas, worsen the fear of an already nervous person, irrational though it is.

The surgeon was thoughtful, and in order to dispel people's fear he always made a point of joking about his initials. As a patient was being prepared for an operation he'd go along and laughingly say to them, "Now forget all about your groundless fear. My initials 'B.F.' don't stand for what you think they do. They stand for Butterfingers."

Another surgeon had a name that blatantly reminded patients of what was coming to them. It was Cutright. He was eventually persuaded to get it changed ... John, have you ever heard of Doctor Cutwrong?

Jane, you've probably sensed the embarrassment of some young men with leg injuries at having to take their trousers off in your presence. I was glad to stand with my trousers off in front of a nurse, just to overcome the inhibition. It wasn't for long, because she'd got to get back on duty.

Your dad, Jane, spoke about advice on marriage, and as he and your mother have enjoyed a happy relationship without difficulty let me tell you something about a couple less fortunate.

There was a favourite piece of advice given by a marriage guidance counsellor for restoring the togetherness of the two partners. One couple explained to her that their nerves were so shattered by their unruly gang of children that they constantly bickered at each other. The counsellor trotted out her standard cure for that sort of hostility − "Think of what it is that you both like doing best, and do it together." They said, "We have done. That's how we got all the kids."

I know it's a bit cruel of me, but before I finish I must throw in a morsel from Jane and John's courtship. In its infancy, before it had become public knowledge, one of the lads happened to see the two of them walking down a lane, holding hands. He told the rest of us about it and when we next met up with Jane we said, (TEASINGLY) "We know all about you and John down that lane the other evening!"

Poor Jane was so flustered, and she said, "I only kissed him!"

One lad said, "That isn't what we heard!"

(BEND TO LOOK AT NOTES. DURING THE FOLLOWING, LOOSEN UP PHYSICALLY, LOOKING AROUND AND BENDING FORWARD TO MAKE A COMING GLANCE AT YOUR NOTES APPEAR NATURAL)

Ladies and gentlemen, I see that I've come to the final item in my notes, and my closing words are to be an acknowledgement of John's appreciation of the barmaids. (IGNORE ANY REACTION TO THIS)

As much as I agree with his assessment of their appeal, in my opinion this was quite the wrong day to make such saucy and suggestive comments to them. (BEND FORWARD, EYES HAPPEN TO LIGHT ON NOTES AGAIN, SOME HESITATION, A CLOSER LOOK TAKEN, THEN ABJECTLY) Ladies and gentlemen, I do apologise. I'd got here "B APOSTROPHE MAIDS" — "B'MAIDS" — and of course it stands for "BRIDESMAIDS", not "BARMAIDS". I'm so sorry. (TO JOHN) I'm sorry about that, John.

Dear bridesmaids, I agree with John about you also, and John, on their behalf, I thank you for your nice remarks and your good wishes.

Now, what I've said apropos the bridesmaids couldn't be more sincere, unlike some of the fibs I've told.

Jane and John, thank you for being such good sports and listening to my shocking slander.

The best of luck to a fine medical team!

BEST MAN No. 15
(Relates to Bridegroom's speech no. 13, on page 104.)

May I say something first of all in all seriousness. I thought John gave an excellent summary of himself just now. He put himself in a nutshell, and many a one in the past would have liked to put him in a nutshell — and leave him there.

I've been a first-hand observer of John for a long time, being a close friend of his, and I've been drawn into many of his wild schemes as an unwilling ally. His ventures were always *adventures*. He was always after the fast buck, but it was too fast and he couldn't catch it.

He was in his element when he'd fastened onto a new idea, no matter how harebrained the idea was. We've all witnessed a church wedding today, and as it was John's it reminded me that even the church was not untouched when it came to his business initiative.

It struck him that many a young couple getting married had to watch every pound they spent, especially if circumstances were such that there was little parental financial back-up. John worked on the idea of a cheap package wedding. To start with, the wedding would be a closely guarded secret to minimise the cost of the reception, so the congregation would be few in number.

John put an experiment into operation and a dummy wedding was set up. Although it was an economy wedding, everything as far as possible was to appear normal.

It started with the Wedding March and I noticed that the organist was playing with greatly exaggerated movements and swaying about. When I pointed this out to John, he said, "That's not an organist. That's the bridegroom. The music's being played on tape".

When the bride walked up the aisle, I said, "Why is her father wearing bicycle clips!" It was because he was also her chauffeur.

The vicar's voice boomed, but there was no sign of him. Everything was on tape. After he announced a hymn there was a pause filled with coughing and spluttering, and then the organ let fly again, and an invisible congregation straggled into the first verse, and when they'd got under way, half of them were out of tune. John explained that everything was designed to be authentic.

It sounded such a large congregation on the tape, and I suggested to John that some couples preferred a quiet wedding. He said, "Well, all they have to do is turn the sound down."

The trickiest part was the best man having to double as chief bridesmaid.

Because almost anything triggered off John's single-minded enthusiasm, no matter how absurd it seemed, whenever I suggested a ridiculous idea in fun, he took me seriously — and there was no stopping him until he'd pursued the idea to its profitless end.

The best example was when I said, "You know, John, you should capitalise on all your business experience. You could write one of those booklets on a multitude of different ways of making money."

He didn't take this as sarcasm, so I followed up by pointing out that his book would be different, because it would deal with enterprises that he'd tried and tested, and which other people might think of. He could explain in each case why it failed. This would save people all the time and fruitless expense of trying the projects out themselves.

John could really go to town with the advertisement — "SAVE TIME AND MONEY — DETAILS OF 100 UNSUCCESSFUL ENTERPRISES".

When it was all over I said to John, "It's a pity that your most dismal failure wasn't included in the booklet." He said, "What was that?" I said, "Writing a booklet on a hundred unsuccessful enterprises."

When John met Jane, he met his match in more than one way. One thing she was certain about was the sincerity of his early protestations of his love for her. He would go down on one knee (one of hers, of course) and plead, "I yearn for you! ... I yearn for you! ... I *yearn* for you! ... You don't know how much I yearn!" She said, "I do — six pound an hour and double time on Sundays.''

John, you triumphed in the most important enterprise of all — your courtship of Jane.

To finish, I'll perform my pleasant duty of thanking you, John, on behalf of the bridesmaids, for your good wishes for them. Thank you.

SPOOF TELEMESSAGES

After making his speech the best man has the pleasant duty of reading out the congratulations from well-wishers who are unable to be present.

Often there are many of these, usually in the form of brief 'telemessages' and if a few of them are witty, then no problem. But what if there are very few, or there are a lot but they are boring? Well, no harm in adding a few of your own to brighten things up! You can get away with it because the groom's side think they must be from the bride's friends and relations, and vice versa!

Here is the sort of thing I mean:

1. Sorry we haven't got you a gift yet. You know how forgetful I am. Happy birthday. Love from Alice and ... you know — Thingy.

2. Hope your marriage proves more straightforward than ours. See you after recovery from the sex change op. Love from Auntie Graham and Uncle Edith.

3. (STUDY MESSAGE FOR A MOMENT BEFORE SPEAKING) I'm sure some of these have come to the wrong wedding party, you know.
    To Heinrich und Ilse. Best vishes fur your life together in Leipzig. Mit love from Uncle Fritz und Auntie Eva.

4. Hope you have as large a family as we did. Love from Sarah and Tom, and Bill, Alan, John, Doris, Alec, Pearl, Jim, Sue, Joan, Eddie, Edwina, Bob, Angie, Brian, Norma, Molly, Kate, Miranda, Chris, Alice, Tony, Rachel, Joanne, Jill, Joy, Dave, Matthew, Simon, Louise, Dawn, Jackie, Pat, Nigel, Jonathan, Jeanne, Joe, Margaret, Connie, Fred, June,

Alexander, Peter, Madeline, Jennifer, Sam, Cedric, Celia, Cecil, Darren, Derren, Dolly, Silly Sandra, ... (LOOK CLOSELY) ... No, sorry — Sally, Sandra, Stewart, Cynthia, Stan, Humphrey, Hubert, Harold and the twins.

5. (FOR A ROMAN CATHOLIC WEDDING)
    Sorry that I couldn't perform the ceremony. Father (NAME OF PRIEST WHO TOOK THE WEDDING CEREMONY) wouldn't change places with me for the day. Blessings from (NAME OF THE POPE).

6. This message is in two parts. The first is for Jane — "I wouldn't change places with you tonight for anything." ... The second is for John — "I *would* change places with you tonight for anything."
                              "Best wishes from Fred."
    (If preferred, the word "tonight" could be omitted.)

7. "Don't forget, dear — the slightest ill-treatment and you come home to mother." ... (CLOSER LOOK) Oh, it's for John.

8. "Best wishes for your future happiness. Please send us each a postcard on your honeymoon. Love from (name of any large group, club or organisation with which the couple have any link)."

9. This one's addressed to Jane — "Best wishes to you and John for your future happiness, from the Under 30's Club." (PICK UP THE NEXT GREETING) And this one's addressed to John — "Best wishes to you and Jane for your future happiness, from the Over 40's Club."

10. (FOR A BRIDEGROOM WHO IS AN ANGLER, BUT NOT PARTICULARY SUCCESSFUL) This is to John. "We've heard about you from your fishing companions. Hearty congratulations on the only good catch you ever made. Love from the Tiddlers."

11. "I know it's very sentimental, but would you name your first

girl after my old granny, who became well known in her
day ... as the Hartlepool Strangler. Love from Alice."

12. (a) "It's a good job you're now man and wife
     − The stork they shot came back to life.
                               Best wishes from Anon."

    (b) "We know the joy a family brings,
         But give us time to rest our wings.
                           Best wishes from the Storks."

    (c) "Some have many, some have few,
         But what a surprise is coming to you!
                          Best wishes from A. Stork."

    (d) Here's one from the Family Planning Association:
         "Our motto is still what it's always been −
         There's more to a stork than margarine."

13. This one says, "A little advice from a worn-out well-wisher:
Don't try to keep up with the Joneses,
You'll find that it doesn't pay −
Especially if they've got fourteen kids,
And another one on the way."

14. "Don't forget you promised to name the first one after
me. Very best wishes for your future health and
happiness from Nebuchadnezzar."

15. This is from the manager of your brand-new
honeymoon hotel.
"Please be patient if there's a minor delay when you
arrive. We're putting something on for you ... It's the
roof."

PART 6
"EXTRA" SPEECHES

"EXTRA" No. 1

Lady friend of family
(from a feminist viewpoint)

I think it fitting that a few things should be said on this occasion from the female viewpoint. I'm not disparaging the comments made by the gentlemen in their speeches. Far from it, because they have been most complimentary to our sex and they've made some flattering observations. I think you ladies will agree that we could listen to that all day. No, it's merely that men do the speechifying at weddings and ladies rarely get a look in — or a word in. It's one more example of men being given priority over women. Even with my humble self being invited to participate, it's still three men to one woman.

Let's hope it's only a matter of time before we ladies break even with the men, and the bride and chief bridesmaid make speeches. Can you imagine a bride standing there in her wedding dress, declaring that she'll still have her night out with the boys every Wednesday and play football on Sundays, and the chief bridesmaid saying how pretty the bridegroom looks? At least they'll have the opportunity to say what they like to a captive audience.

Unfortunately my wedding service was marred by a series of hiccups. They came from Stan, who hadn't recovered from his stag party ... You could tell he was still seeing double. When the vicar said, "Do you take this woman?" he said, "Which woman?" The only way the vicar could get him to say "I will" was to ask him if he'd have another drink. When I was asked if I would take him for better or worse, I thought well, it can't get much worse ... When he signed the register in the vestry it looked as though a bow-legged spider had trodden in some ink and then done the Twist.

Anyway, the point I want to make is the same sort of thing

as the unfairness of the male monopoly of the speechmaking. Did you ever hear of a bride staggering up the aisle singing, "I've got a luvverly bunch of coconuts," because she hasn't sobered up from her hen party? It's all right for men to behave irresponsibly though, isn't it! Any disgraceful spectacle a man makes of himself is treated by other men as a joke.

Well, I've had my little say, and now on the lighter side I can tell you that in spite of everything, the years that have passed since that memorable day that I've just told you about, have been as happy as I could have wished. The toast to Stan and myself has been fulfilled, and I only hope that the good wishes expressed by all of us for Jane and John's future will materialise just the same. I can't say fairer than that.

It's over to you now, Jane and John, to make your married life a happy one. Having the pleasure of knowing you both well, I know in my heart that you will do this. May God's blessing be with you all the way.

"EXTRA" No. 2

Groom's Uncle
(Groom in the car industry)

You've just heard me introduced as John's uncle. For those of you who don't know, I'm his *father's* brother.

Now, when an uncle of the bridegroom is invited to speak at the wedding, it's either because he's a good speaker or he knows his nephew very well. In this case it was for both reasons.

I can tell you that apart from what you can see for yourselves about John — his handsome looks, his intelligent face, his poise, his charm and so on — he's also the most kind, generous, noble, courageous, modest and self-effacing young gentleman that you could imagine.

I could go on in that vein, but you'd think I was indulging in fancy. But I wouldn't be, for this reason. Frank has always said that John takes after me.

I shouldn't have told you that, should I, because it makes it embarrassing for me to extol John's virtues. I'll pass over the finer attributes and pick on a few characteristics here and there.

John's an ambitious young man and in his career in the motor industry he's already carving out a place for himself. He's chosen his firm well. Due to increased demand, they've had to build an enormous extension to their premises ... It's the complaints department.

John asked for a transfer to this department because he wanted the security. Jane, would you bear something in mind, now that you're married to John. When he comes home in the evening, and he's had a hard day, don't complain about anything. If he walks mud all over the carpet, or he's too tired to take you out, whatever it is, say nothing.

I'm advising you this for your own sake as well as his, because it'll be no use complaining. He'll be able to refute your complaint, and you'll get nowhere. As a final resort with a dissatisfied customer he says, "It's your own fault for buying one of our cars in the first place!" If you press things to the limit, he'll only say, "It's your own fault for marrying me in the first place!"

A notable quality of John's is his initiative. To cope with the volume of people coming to complain, they've adopted his suggestion of using an appointment system.

He's been telling me how nasty some of these people can be. I mean, there's no need for sarcasm. You know those posters exhorting drivers to keep danger off the road. He's seen things added, like, "If you bought your car from Runwell's, push it back into your garage."

There's one good point about their service. A customer doesn't have to collect the car himself. They tow it to his home.

Their manufacturers tried out a new system to speed up delivery direct to the customer, but not enough people could follow the assembly instructions.

A free offer sales promotion of theirs didn't work either. On the bonnets it said, "Send in the number plates from ten cars that you buy and you'll get your next one free."

There's obviously plenty of scope for anyone with bright ideas.

John, there's one great thing that you've done that wasn't a bright idea. You've married Jane.

No young man would have to be bright to want to have Jane as a wife. Her worthiness (I nearly said "roadworthiness" — I must forget about cars) is only too obvious.

The best of luck to you both on life's road.

"EXTRA" No. 3
Bride's sister

It's not often that a sister of the bride is given some time to say her piece at the reception. The truth is that I was nudged into it — well, coerced into it really. The reason given was that Jane and I have always been very close. Mind you, I think it was a shaky excuse for getting me on my hind legs, or any other legs, to impose myself on all of you. I suspect that it was done primarily so I wouldn't feel left out and I do appreciate that.

Anyway, as to our Jane, I can tell you that she's always been the active little extrovert that she is now. Some people who have been at the receiving end of her activities would have used different phraseology from mine. I'm thinking of her younger days. In fact, the farther back we go, the worse it gets.

I had the misfortune to be Jane's elder sister. It doesn't take much imagination to know what that can mean. Looking back, I think that people would have described Jane as a mischievous little tomboy. I was supposed to look after her, but while she was around I needed somebody to look after me. There was never a dull moment, and that can cover a multitude of sins.

She played tricks on me that a little boy's supposed to play on his elder sister. I dreaded her answering the 'phone to my boyfriend when I wasn't in. She'd tell him that I'd gone out with another man, if Dad had happened to give me a lift somewhere in the car.

Later on in life you could tell how close we were getting. We even used the same make-up — mine. In a family clothes are usually handed down. Mine weren't. They were taken. (TO JANE) Do you remember all this, Jane?

It's a funny thing that you can assume that a person has the same image of themselves as a child that someone else in the house has of them. I wonder if Jane thinks I'm painting a false picture of her. I'll balance things up by disclosing the credit side.

I was immature in my sister's earlier years, and failed to see that what I thought was naughtiness was, in fact, merely devilment. It takes all sorts to make a world. (That's a telling statement to make in someone's defence, isn't it?)

Without the Janes, the world would be a duller place — and indeed a poorer place in many respects. Jane's energies have already done more good in the world than most people achieve in a lifetime. She may have taken delight in mischievous tricks in her childhood, but by the same token she takes delight in springing pleasant surprises on people.

From dropping me in it with earlier boyfriends, she's cleverly smoothed things over with later ones, especially with the one I married, and that's probably news to him.

I spoke of the world being a poorer place without its Janes, and my own particular world would have been poorer without this particular Jane. We were close in the past, we remained close when I married, and we'll still be close now that she's married.

"EXTRA" No. 4

Bride

It's nice to have this opportunity to speak to everybody at once. I wasn't really prepared for it. It was Ken's bright idea. He sprung it on me only a few days ago, when I'd got enough to think about without giving my mind to a speech.

I gave him a flat refusal at first because of the short notice. Mind you, I gave John a flat refusal when he first proposed to me, and yet here I am.

It was afterwards that I began to think that if I only spoke briefly it would be an opportunity to thank all of you for the congratulations and good wishes for John and myself. Then there's all the help that I've had one way or another in preparing for the big day. There are too many names to name.

Those who haven't been closely involved in the run-up have helped with moral support. I never knew what a difference it would make getting married with everybody's blessing. It's made it so much happier, and I do thank you for that.

John has thanked his parents for putting up with him for twenty years or so. (TO JOHN) How old are you, by the way, John?

He's also kindly acknowledged what my mum and dad have done, and I'd like to second that.

I couldn't do justice to thanking my parents for a lifetime of care and love in the short time at my disposal. Suffice it to say that whatever I've done, they've stuck by me through thick and thin, especially when I went on a diet.

I want to thank John's mum and dad for bringing him into the world and giving me something that I can get my teeth into … I don't mean love bites. He doesn't quite know what he's let himself in for yet.

Perhaps I could single out somebody (or somebodies) for my own praise, because they are very young people and they've done a special service. You'll know who I mean — and they do, they're beaming away already — my darling bridesmaids.

I think that's about all, unless I can publicly thank John for asking me to marry him for the thirteenth time.

Well, marriage shouldn't be rushed into, should it? It's my opinion that a couple need at least three weeks to get to know each other. I think I knew John well enough after a fortnight, but I was afraid that he didn't really know me, so it was for his own protection that I declined for the first twelve times. By the thirteenth time we both knew something more about each other. I knew how persistent he could be and he knew how obstinate I could be.

Well, thank you all again for everything. John's already given you our thanks for your generous gifts. They really have added to our excitement.

Thank you for listening, and now I'll let you carry on enjoying yourselves.

"EXTRA" No. 5

Son of bride
(Bride's second marriage)

Sue and I have been getting some reactions of surprise and disbelief when we've had occasion to say to people insufficiently acquainted with us, "My Mum's getting married."

I suppose it does sound odd coming out just like that. People almost stand back and stare as though they're trying to re-judge our ages, as if their first impression was wildly wrong and they were twenty years out. You could almost see the unspoken thought, such as "She's left it a bit late, hasn't she?" What we should have said was, "My Mum's remarrying."

You see, our mum and dad had lived in a different era — one of order instead of disorder — and they were among those parents who succeeded in keeping that ideal alive for their children. We're conditioned to thinking in terms of the orderliness of family life, that's why we've trotted out that statement in all innocence, without thought of its immediate implication in most people's minds.

It was a devastating blow when we lost Dad, but time has done its healing work even though there has remained a gap in the family. There are Dad's brothers and sisters amongst us, here to celebrate Mum's union with a new partner, Les, so I'm sure that Les won't feel any discomfort if I pay homage to Dad, and let them know that we do not forget him.

I spoke of a gap in the family, and if I say that the family is now rounded out again, it isn't a reference to Les's shape.

Les is one of Mum's generation and he shares her outlook. I suppose this is what brings middle-aged people together. If Les hadn't been like this, I think that Sue and I would have regarded him as a stranger in the camp, as we are both still living with Mum.

There is more than mere rapport between us and Les. There is an understanding and mateyness that promises well for a happy household.

Of course, if he does try to come the heavy-handed father, it will be a different matter. We've made secret plans for if he sends us to bed early or stops our pocket money.

There will be some changes in the division of labour now that Mum's taken on a new hand. As the new man of the house, it will fall to him, for example, to dig the garden and take Mum shopping in the car, as a dutiful husband should. Notice that I did say "for example."

Come what may, I hereby wish Mum and Les a very happy future together.

"EXTRA" No. 6
Groom's godmother

Some of you may not know why I've been singled out to chip in on the speechmaking. It's because I'm John's godmother. Not his fairy godmother, I'm five stone too heavy for that.

As his godmother it's been my duty to encourage him to attend church. Today I am proud to say that I finally made it.

I'll tell you one thing. It's refreshing to attend a good, old-fashioned church wedding where the couple are people you belong with. Jane and John have made a good start.

There's too much cynicism around these days. Mind you, there always has been about marriage and the cynics are usually men. I tried to cheer up a fellow who was disillusioned after his marriage. I said, "Look, you've got to expect some bad times as well as all the good. Clouds can come over your married life, but all clouds pass on."

He looked even more despondent, so I said, "What's the matter?" He said, "My mother-in-law shows no sign of passing on."

Then there was the conversation between two businessmen

who'd just met. One invited the other to a good night out that he was planning for his pals. A miserable look came over the other's face and he said, "I can't come. All that week I shall be down at Brighton, shacked up with my secretary." The first chap said, "Well, ... why are you looking so depressed about that?" He said, "I've been married to her for forty years."

That reminds me of a cartoon where a very stout, formidable-looking woman had entered her husband's office, crept up behind him and placed her hands over his eyes. The little chap was grinning and giggling away and saying, "Not now, darling, I'm expecting the wife any minute."

Nowadays a good many young women are rebelling against the idea of being married. They want to pursue careers instead of trying to find change for the kids' dinner money.

Happy are they who can combine career and marriage ... Wouldn't you be happy if you'd performed a miracle? Where the couple have young children it can seem like one. It's a matter of skilful planning.

Jane is continuing with her career, but she hopes for welcome interruptions to it.

May she have the best of both worlds, and I can look forward to seeing John in church again for a christening. This time, not his own.

"EXTRA" No. 7

I've been asked to say a few words because I know one half of today's happy couple so well. By "happy couple" I'm not referring to John's parents because of their relief at getting him off their hands. They are a happy couple and they probably are relieved to get him off their hands, but it's John himself that I'm talking about.

He and I are cousins and because of our closeness in age we made good companions in our early years and this friendship continued through boyhood into manhood, so we know each other pretty well. It's a strange thought, I find, that you know someone far better than the person they've just married knows them.

Before that thought discomforts you, Jane, I hasten to assure you that there's nothing too terrible about your husband that you don't already know. Terrible, yes, but not too terrible. In fact, I congratulate you on getting him to the altar ... That's not a reflection on you! It's a knock at him!

Phew! Isn't it difficult sometimes to say something without the meaning being open to misconstruction! I've heard of speakers being told to put a sock in it, but a speech itself can be like a sock. It's all too easy to put your foot in it. Can I change my mind, Ken, and not do this after all?

(BACK TO GUESTS) I'll concentrate on the safe subject, now — John himself. I'd like to give his in-laws particularly, a sketch of his character. They must be interested to hear about him first-hand from somebody who won't sugar the pill.

John can be a puzzle to the newcomer in his life because he's full of surprises. For one thing, he's absent-minded in some ways. Jane, you'll be interested in this. He's the sort of chap who'll never forget his wedding anniversary, but he'll forget who he's married to. If you dye your hair yellow he might notice, but he won't remember what colour it was before.

I've known him come to our house in the winter and we've asked him if it's cold out, and he's gone back outside again to find out.

In some spheres his academic attainment has been extraordinary. One school report for maths said he was well away with trigonometry, but he couldn't get the hang of long division. For his summing up his form master said he was a pupil who couldn't be summed up.

He distinguished himself one sports day, but unfortunately there were spiteful rumours about drug-taking — just because he came third in the egg-and-spoon race.

Jane, you're the important one because it's you that's just married the chap, and there's an all-important characteristic possessed by John that you inevitably know by now as well as I do. That's his good nature. He's been a true friend to me and he'll make a loyal and loving husband for you.

Good luck to you both.

"EXTRA" No. 8
Bride's mother

As I have the wisdom that comes from experience twenty-five years after my wedding, I'd like to pass a few tips on to Jane. It will give me a chance to carry on about men in general and Frank in particular.

Jane dear, husbands think they're the superior ones, on whom wives depend for their security and protection. This is a myth that originates in the image of a Stone Age man wielding a club to clout dangerous animals at the mouth of the family cave. The only resemblance that your dad has borne to such a specimen is when he's gone for a time without shaving or getting his hair cut, and his club is a place where he spends too much time drinking with his cronies.

If you stop and think about it, which sex is better at survival? If a man's away from home for a week or two the wife can get by with the man's jobs, but you look at the mess a man gets into when his wife goes into hospital for a spell.

He can be hopeless at taking the woman's place, as witness what our neighbour told me about your dad when I was away having you. He had no idea how to peep through curtains without being seen. She called in for a friendly chat over a cup of tea, but he couldn't enter into the spirit of it. He hadn't a bad word to say about anybody.

(TO GUESTS) Apparently he overreached himself with his efforts at cooking. Our neighbour spotted something in the kitchen that she thought was a clever piece of work. She said, "Did you make that yellow model of a skyscraper?" He said, "Something went wrong. That was supposed to be a pancake."

I don't know whether it was plain ignorance or whether he was just being sarcastic about me, but he said he didn't think the vacuum cleaner worked unless you had haircurlers in.

Really, I think if he were a bride, he'd get to the church on time.

Men are good at their own things, of course, like forgetting their wife's birthday and saying the wrong thing in public. When Frank forgot my last birthday and I was telling a friend about it, he said very timidly, "No, I didn't forget, dear. When you were fifty you said you weren't having them any more."

I wouldn't have minded so much, but I was only thirty-six ... or round about that. It was only one figure out. I was forty-six.

This isn't the first time that I've warned Jane about what can lie ahead after the wedding. I've drummed things into her, but John, my dear, in spite of all, she's cheerfully gone ahead and married you. That means that you must be something special.

She's a lucky girl, John, and you're a lucky lad. May luck remain with you both when Jane's no longer a girl and you're no longer a lad.

"EXTRA" No. 9

Son of divorced or widowed groom

First of all I should like to welcome Brenda into the family. I hope that she finds us as amenable as we find her. We've got along well so far, but when the honeymoon's over and unfortunately she gets to know us better, well ... let's just hope that she can tolerate us.

The word "amenable" applied to Brenda, I'm afraid I used thoughtlessly, because she is much more than that. It's how she's going to find us lot that I'm worried about.

You see, Brenda, if you were coming to the house during the engagement, Dad would make us hide all the empty beer cans and tidy up. Then he'd give us a clout round the ear and say, "And just behave yourselves when Brenda comes!"

The instant the bell rang Dad would say, "She's 'ere! Get yer feet off the table!" and he'd be at the door like a shot. Then he'd reappear in a state of anti-climax mumbling irritably, "How many more times do they need telling! We don't *want* double glazing!"

However, when Dad went to the door and we heard, (USE APPROPRIATE VOICE) "Come in, dear," we knew that either Dad had had a sudden change of mind and the latest double glazing salesman was in luck, or it was you.

As it happened, each time it was you. Dad would be going on, "You must be very cold," or "You must be very hot," or "You must be very wet," or "You must be very dry," ... It was like getting a weather report. Anyway you were very welcome.

Then we had to watch our "p's" and "q's" − or, more to the point, our "b's" and "c's". Thankfully we managed to curb our language, in spite of the force of habit.

After Dad had first met you, we got wind of something, and as the eldest son, it fell to me to assert authority. I would say to Dad, before he went out in the evening, "Now, I'm not prying. You're old enough to live your own life and have your fling, but just make sure you're back home by nine o'clock."

But you know how difficult parents can be today. He came home in his own sweet time. I used to say to him, "My father wouldn't have allowed me to stop out at all hours. I was brought up strictly."

Brenda, he's your responsibility now. You will have to try and keep a check on him. However, with all Dad's anxiety to make a good impression on you, well, it's a measure of his esteem for you, isn't it? And your magnetic charm will hold him.

We, his family, are over the moon that Dad has won you, and we wish you both the very best of happiness.

"EXTRA" No. 10

Middle-aged male friend or relative
(Relates to Bride's Father speech no. 8, on page 29.)

Frank has had something to say about changing attitudes, and how right he is! I know of a girl whose mother was shocked when she moved in with her boyfriend. She said to the girl, "If your great-great-great-grandmother were alive, I don't know what she'd say!" The girl replied, "Probably —'Look at me. I'm a hundred and thirty and I'm not dead yet!' "

That's an attitude prevalent among young people today.

Now, I know that Jane and John have already had a few years' experience of the marriage situation, but couples long married can run into trouble with each other, as we all know. Separations and divorces happen at almost any age. I say "almost" because you don't often hear of a pair in their eighties getting divorced. That's probably because they can't afford it out of their pension. On the other hand they may take the line, "We've put up with each other for all this time, it's hardly worth splitting up now."

So I make no apology for offering our happy couple some secondhand advice.

A basic cause of marriage breakdown is that as the newlyweds become oldyweds, the romance that attached them together fades. In their earliest days a young couple may live under a spell which makes them kindly disposed to one another, come what may. They fall over themselves to be tolerant. But when the spell goes, that goes. I'm telling Jane and John this because, whether they know it or not, they're still in the enchanted land, and it's as well for them to be prepared for when they come out of it.

The secret is to maintain tolerance.

I recall a sketch on the stage where an extremely agitated young man was waiting outside a cinema for his fiancée, who was very late. When she did arrive, he flung his arms round her with a sigh of relief and poured out his fears of what might have happened to her.

The second part of the sketch showed the same situation thirty years later. You can imagine how their love had mellowed into something rich and tender. When the woman turned up late, the man stepped forward, took her hand in his, twisted her arm up her back and said, (FIERCELY) "Where've yer bin?!"

At present John probably sits gazing at Jane across the breakfast table, lost in admiration and blissfully unconscious of his teeth fighting a losing battle with some bread that by a miracle has been transformed into charcoal. Time could change that to, (FIERCELY) "We've been married for what seems ninety years and you still burn the toast!"

So, my young friends, discipline yourselves to be tolerant, and whenever you clash, don't get your backs up at each other, but talk things over. Some neighbours of mine do that regularly. I can hear them from three doors away.

Jane and John, it feels good to me to have this opportunity to wish you both, with family and friends all listening, every bit of luck that you deserve as truly man and wife.

"EXTRA" No. 11

Older male friend of groom

I've known John since before he started going out with girls. He used to go about in a pram. If he encountered a little girl he used to gurgle at her. What he gurgled, when translated, was "Does your mother know you're out?"

It's no secret that Jane is the last in a very long line of the opposite sex that have engaged John's attention ... well, it might have been a secret from Jane, but it isn't now.

Eventually an influential little fellow took a hand in John's life. His name is Cupid, and he stalks the realms of bachelorhood with safety because he's invisible — and so are his arrows. You can't see them coming, otherwise you could duck.

This happened to John, but fortunately it was Jane who was on the scene. Cupid aimed an arrow at John's heart and scored a bull's-eye. His shots are not always good because he fires balancing on one leg. This can have the opposite effect of what was intended. Even if a young man is struck, he might not get a pain in the heart over a girl, but instead find her a pain in the something else. It's no wonder he's sometimes shown blindfolded.

It's a pity that Cupid's invisible, because from what I've seen of his pictures we could have him arrested for streaking.

At least he's put a stop to John's little gallop. John should only get one Valentine card next time, not dozens. If he does get more than one, there's still only one that he'll be able to display. And there's only one that he'll buy. In the past he's had them at cut price for buying in bulk.

John's practice of spreading his net wide caused him some problems. Sometimes when he got home his mum or dad would say, "Oh, by the way, your girlfriend phoned." He'd say, "Did she give her name?"

You should have seen his address book with all the girls' telephone numbers in ... or perhaps you shouldn't if you understand hieroglyphics. It's the first address book I've ever known that needed an "X" certificate.

There was an episode when John resorted to deceit. Some of his friends were dying to know what a graphologist would see in his handwriting about his flirtatious nature. They kidded John to join with them in submitting samples. It puzzled them why he agreed, until they saw the graphologist's report on him — "This person is a lecherous young man who thinks he can disguise his handwriting."

When he was only a little chap he was trying to sort out in his mind how many girls had succumbed to his charms. He was pulling the legs off a centipede and going, (FROWN THOUGHTFULLY AND ACT THIS OUT, PUTTING DOWN ON ONE SIDE AND THEN THE OTHER) "*She* loves me ... *she* loves me not ... *she* loves me ... *she* loves me not ..."

John, people say that marriage brings its complications. It can't bring you any more complications than you had before you settled on Jane.

My wish is quite uncomplicated. It's simply for the best of happiness for you both.

"EXTRA" No. 12

Bride
(Divorced, remarrying after a long time)

As you know, I've been married before, but my first wedding reception was in the days before female emancipation and I wasn't invited to speak. Even chaining myself to some railings didn't do the trick. The irony of it was that I only wanted to point out that I admired men so much that I was marrying one of them.

There's a saying that we all know well enough — "Only a fool makes the same mistake twice." I'm not making the same mistake twice, or even a different mistake, in marrying John. This couldn't be the same as my first mistake (and it was a mistake) because my fault was in marrying before I was ready for marriage.

I was so shaken by my own blunder that it frightened me off a future union for longer than some young people here have been around. You could say that my second mistake was in not getting married for all that length of time.

Although I say it myself, I was not without suitors throughout my long "I want to be alone" period. One of them's here today, and that's John.

So what brought that era to a close? Basically it was the gentleman that I've just mentioned. Unlike the others, he wouldn't go away when he was told to. I think that was because I didn't tell him as determinedly as I had told the others. It wasn't because I was becoming exhausted, fending off an endless succession of ardent admirers, but because the phase had run its course. My defences were down.

There were three parties whose concerted efforts finally broke through the barrier. One, of course, was John himself, because, let's face it, I wouldn't marry just anybody simply because I was no longer afraid to marry. That would have been foolhardy.

The second party is plural. Some of my friends had dropped subtle hints, such as, "Why don't you get married again?" — after John had come into my life. I've given it away there, haven't I, saying "into my life". It's a telling expression.

The third party was Old Father Time. He was nudging things along, saying, "Enough is enough."

Well, thank you, John, for coming along just when the time was ripe. You weren't just anybody at the right time, you were the right man at the right time.

Thank you, also, all my genuine friends who have kept me happy throughout the many years of my single life. This is my opportunity also to thank you for sharing in my happiness in finding John, and for all your thoughtfulness in so many ways.

Old Father Time, I thank you as well, but please keep your nose out of things now. John and I want to savour our life, not have it hurried on.

Thank you, everyone, for joining our celebration, and for all your kind wishes.

"EXTRA" No. 13

Daughter of divorced bride

I've been without a father for most of my life. Mum's been without a husband for most of my life. Mum can remember what it's like to have a husband, but I've forgotten what it's like to have a father.

To be truthful, I should say that I *had* forgotten, because lately I have been reminded. Things are coming back to me from the dim and distant past. Having a man about the house quite a lot has stirred childhood memory.

At the same time there are wide differences between the man in my infancy and the new one. The new one is so young! A dad to me at one time was somebody big and tall and old. My new dad, as John now is, is somebody reduced to a manageable size.

The first dad used to send me to bed early if I misbehaved. If this one tries anything like that, he's more likely to be frightened when I stamp my foot in temper.

This seems a good opportunity to give him fair warning. I've been mentally listing the things that will be different in this second father régime. For a start I shall want my pocket money doubled. I shall expect ten pence a week instead of the five I had before!

Mum, I hope you will make it clear to John that he does not have to hold my hand when I cross the road. That's another thing that will be different.

There is something that I shall be interested to see when John is settled in. Will he still buy you flowers and other gifts, or was that all a ruse to trap you into marriage, and something that he will drop now that you've signed on as what he thinks is a cleaner and a cook and general dogsbody, whose function, in short, is to be his slave? Why else does he keep sneaking looks at those photographs of women?

(BACK TO GUESTS) He's got a whole album of them that he thinks we don't know about, called "What women are best for," and they're all on the same theme. They're all poor, downtrodden housewives slaving over hot stoves, scrubbing floors, doing piles of washing and ironing and mending … It's disgusting!

But he'll get his comeuppance. He'd have a shock if he saw the photographs of men that Mum has. They're all of poor, downtrodden husbands slaving over hot stoves, scrubbing floors, doing piles of washing and ironing and mending … It's glorious!

You see, John, we can tell you now. *You*'ve signed on as cleaner, cook and general dogsbody, whose function, in short, is to be our slave all the time that you're not out earning our keep. Protest will be useless. But it will be worth your while!

"EXTRA" No. 14

Friend of groom
(Groom a car enthusiast)

To me the one thing about John that has been most colourful is his enthusiasm for motor cars and motoring.

Although I want to enlighten you about this, I don't want you to think that the one great joy of John's life is driving his car. An equal joy is leaving it where it says, "NO PARKING".

John is one of those mechanical geniuses that leave unpractical dolts like myself lost in wonder and disbelief at their achievements. He can actually build up a motor car for next to nothing from spare parts and bits and pieces of junk from anywhere that he can lay his hands on them or scrounge them. Mind you, (NAME OF CAR MANUFACTURERS) do that (OR "used to do that") all the time, but that's another story.

John's even had a go at designing totally new models. There was one he called "The Crab" — but who wants a car that only goes sideways?

I've often wondered what John would have done if he'd lived before the car was invented. Probably he would have invented it. Otherwise I can see him getting his horse out of the stable every Sunday morning and polishing it. Then he'd go galloping down the highway at eighty miles an hour.

I've shared a few crazy motoring experiences with him. Once there were seventeen of us squashed together in a car, whizzing like mad down a motorway. I said, "Slow down a bit, John!" ... Nothing happened, so I repeated, "Slow down a bit, John!" ... Still nothing happened, so I said, "John, for heaven's sake, slow down!" John said, "Blimey! I thought *you* were driving!"

Between us we managed to stop the vehicle altogether — by ramming it into the back of a police car. A policeman who came peering in at the window couldn't believe his eyes when he saw how many there were of us crammed inside. He said, "Which one of you was driving?" John said, "None of us. We were all in the back."

Jane's had her share, too. The police now regard John as a prime target for swift action. He once parked his car at a bus stop while he nipped into a shop. When he came out it was gone. He said to a man in the bus queue, "Did you see what happened to my car?" The man said, "The police towed it away." John looked around and then said, "Did you see where the young lady passenger went?" The man said, "She was still inside it."

Dealing with the likes of John has led traffic wardens to plan a correction centre, called "NO PARKINGHURST". The treatment will be psychological. The inmates' uniforms will be an unusual colour. Every morning they will stand in two long rows so that they form a double yellow line.

In the games room they can play "Monopoly", but a small alteration will be found. When they pick up a card it will say, "YOU HAVE PARKED ILLEGALLY, GO TO GAOL FOR TEN YEARS." A propaganda film will show a motorist committing a parking offence being attacked by an angry crowd.

In conclusion, may I offer just one piece of advice to you, Jane, to ensure that your marriage chugs along peacefully. Never become a traffic warden.

"EXTRA" No. 15

Friend of groom
(Groom a practical joker)

Some of us here are aware, from bitter experience, that John is a practical joker. It can make you ill at ease to be out with him. You never know when anything that he suggests to you has an ulterior motive.

One cold day I went to his house with a Scottish friend, and when John was making some tea, he called to my friend, "Would you like anything in it? I've got something to warm the cockles of a Scots heart." When my friend had drunk all his tea, there was a fifty-pence piece in the bottom of the cup.

He once saw a most outrageous jacket for sale as he was hurrying back to work after his lunch break. He phoned the shop from work and said, "I saw that jacket in your window. What time do you stay open till?" They said, "Five o'clock." He said, "Thank God for that. I don't leave work till half past."

He really confuses people. When he was on a committee organising a bonfire night and the fifth of November fell on a Tuesday, he said, "If it rains on the Tuesday, shall we hold it on the Monday or the Wednesday?"

Do you know, John even took advantage of the confidentiality of the Roman Catholic confessional. He had to say ten "Hail Mary's" for booby-trapping the Vatican.

He was outside a church for a very long time when he was on holiday in Lancashire. There was a big notice board up, saying, "WHERE WILL YOU BE ON JUDGMENT DAY?" John wrote underneath, "WAITING FOR A BUS TO BLACKPOOL."

He'd booked up at a holiday camp. The advertisement in the newspaper said, "No dogs," so he took his own.

I felt sorry for a poor old dear where we stayed for one holiday and there was a lot of mist. He wrote in the visitors' book,

"Glorious views. On a clear day you can see the landlady."

He even put an advertisement in a newspaper offering holiday accommodation with extensive all-round views and only two minutes from the sea. When people wrote in for details, he said it was in the top of a lighthouse.

Well, today's the day for John to be at the receiving end of such trickery, as from when he and Jane start off on their journey. John's done a bit of that on a bridegroom himself. A flight was delayed while Britannia Airways detached all the tin cans from the tail of an aeroplane.

As you're a connoisseur of this sort of thing, John, don't expect anything banal like finding your car without any wheels. You're more likely to find your wheels without any car.

As likely as not there'll be something more subtle. I don't want to give the game away, but there could have been some skulduggery when you signed the register in the vestry. Some time in the future you might discover that you're not really married.

However, don't let that spoil things. May you and Jane carry on now as if you were married, and be happy.

THE BEST MAN'S DUTIES

If you've been asked to be the best man at a wedding and aren't sure what the task entails you need **The Best Man's Duties**.

This comprehensive guide describes in detail *all* the duties expected of a best man. These include being the master of ceremonies, chief marshal in charge of the ushers, toastmaster, paymaster, messenger, persuader, remembrancer, peace-maker, chief liaison officer between the bridegroom and the bridal contingent – as well as a repository for such valuables as the wedding ring, cash, documents for the honeymoon and lost property.

This book will answer all your queries and help you to ensure that the wedding is a great success.

WEDDING ETIQUETTE PROPERLY EXPLAINED

An invaluable handbook covering everything the bride and groom need to know when preparing for their wedding: the legal requirements, the banns, the details of the church service, planning the reception, the catering arrangements, plus much more.

SAMPLE SOCIAL SPEECHES

Sample speeches for every social occasion, including weddings. Also contains information on how to prepare and deliver a speech, as well as lots of anecdotes, aphorisms and stories for you to include in your speech.

THE PUBLIC SPEAKER'S JOKE BOOK

The ideal book for the public speaker. It contains jokes for every occasion: business functions, conventions, dinners, weddings, even children's parties. With over 500 jokes to choose from, you'll never be lost for a humorous quip.

THE RIGHT JOKE FOR THE RIGHT OCCASION

The 615 jokes are listed alphabetically under subject to help you find the right joke for your particular speech. There's also a Directory which provides instant reference to jokes covering hundreds of different subjects.